'Bold, insightful, gospel centred an  reader to consider honestly the st stop. Pete Nicholas argues boldly a to our social ills is not gaining more what we have lost; we have lost God. Brilliant book: every thought leader should get hold of it.'
Girma Bishaw, pastor and Director and founder, The Gratitude Initiative

'After thirty years of speaking at university missions, I have drawn on scores, if not hundreds, of articles and books that are useful in arguing why the Christian faith is so relevant to post-modern Western culture. More recently, I have listened to Pete Nicholas delivering such talks before live audiences and admired both the substance of his material and the style in which he relates to the audience. At last, his outstanding material has been captured in writing and I thoroughly commend it to you. Here are two very practical reasons why: first, if you want to grasp the answers to some big questions about the meaning of life, this is a "go to"; second, if you ever deliver talks on these issues, throw away (most of) your notes and use this book! *A Place for God* is top class. Buy it!'
Graham Daniels, General Director, Christians in Sport

'Before we begin the necessary work of cultural rebuilding, we need to check the foundations and discern whether they are strong enough to build upon. *A Place for God* is a fantastic guide for such an exploration. For those searching for faith or wanting to strengthen their faith, I couldn't recommend this book more highly.'
Pete Hughes, KXC Church, London

'An interesting, creative and deftly woven exploration of life's big questions, and the stories we tell in order to answer them when God has been removed from the town square of our lives. A must read if

you're exploring these questions yourself or know someone who is.'
Kristi Mair, apologist and author of *MORE>Truth: Searching for certainty in an uncertain world*

'Many will recognize themselves in Pete Nicholas's acute analysis of a contemporary world which is not at ease with itself. He combines his description of the symptoms with a fresh and engaging presentation of the Christian faith as both the ultimate explanation of our problems and the fulfilment of our longings. Whatever your faith or lack of it, I guarantee this book will get you thinking – and it could just change your life.'
Vaughan Roberts, pastor and author

A PLACE FOR GOD

Pete Nicholas is a pastor at Inspire Saint James Church, Clerkenwell, London, and the author of *Virtually Human: Flourishing in a Digital World* (IVP) and *Five Things to Pray for Your City* (The Good Book Company). After studying Philosophy, Politics and Economics at the University of Oxford, Pete went on to achieve a Master's in Industrial Relations (also at Oxford) and a Diploma in Theology. He is a regular speaker at events and university missions around the country, writes a regular column for *Evangelicals Now* and is a blog writer for Redeemer City to City (New York) and Christians in Sport.

A PLACE FOR GOD

Navigating timeless questions
for our modern times

Pete Nicholas

INTER-VARSITY PRESS
36 Causton Street, London SW1P 4ST, England
Email: ivp@ivpbooks.com
Website: www.ivpbooks.com

First published 2021

British Library Cataloguing-in-Publication Data
A catalogue record for this book is available from the British Library.

ISBN: 978-1-78974-159-9
eBook ISBN: 978-1-78974-158-2

Set in Minion Pro 10.25/13.75pt
Typeset in Great Britain by CRB Associates, Potterhanworth, Lincolnshire
Printed and bound by CPI Group (UK) Ltd, Croydon CR0 4YY

Produced on paper from sustainable sources

*Inter-Varsity Press publishes Christian books that are true to the Bible and that communicate the
gospel, develop discipleship and strengthen the church for its mission in the world.*

*IVP originated within the Inter-Varsity Fellowship, now the Universities and Colleges Christian
Fellowship, a student movement connecting Christian Unions in universities and colleges
throughout Great Britain, and a member movement of the International Fellowship of Evangelical
Students. Website: www.uccf.org.uk. That historic association is maintained, and all senior IVP
staff and committee members subscribe to the UCCF Basis of Faith.*

For Rebecca,
I can't thank God enough
for such a wonderful partner
on life's pilgrim journey.

Contents

Foreword

Just north of Roosevelt Island, New York, where I've lived for thirty-two years, is a place on the East River called 'Hell Gate'. The name is appropriate because, when the tide comes up from the Atlantic Ocean and meets water coming down the East River, it creates violent, dangerous whirlpools and cross-currents. Many ships caught in Hell Gate have come to grief.

Canadian philosopher Charles Taylor argues that our secular age is not really as secular as advertised, but nor is religion simply marching ahead as in the past. Rather, in our time, both believers and non-believers in God feel strong and sometimes forceful cross-currents or 'cross-pressures'. This means that believers and non-believers are equally likely to be shipwrecked in this Hell Gate.

Believers, of course, are assailed with objections and scepticism from the academy and the media especially, as well as from friends and family. How can a good and all-powerful God allow so much evil? If Christianity is true, how could so many of its followers have been guilty of so much injustice? Why does religion lead to violence? Isn't the Bible filled with regressive social attitudes, historical inaccuracies and contradictions?

However, Taylor shows, non-believers are just as assailed by anxieties and doubts about their own beliefs. They accept what their culture tells them, namely, that intellectually and emotionally mature people don't need to believe in God or the supernatural. But then they find that their secular viewpoint has its own weaknesses when confronting the realities and challenges of human life. The secular belief – that the material world is all that exists – generates its own doubts.

There is the secular doubt about morality: 'Are all moral values really just human social constructions? On what basis, then, can I tell anyone that what they are doing is unjust and plain wrong? Don't I know, deep down, that some things are truly, objectively evil?'

There is the secular doubt about love and beauty: 'Are love and beauty really just what my evolutionary neuro-chemistry finds pleasurable, because it helped my ancestors survive? Fish don't feel out of place in water – so why do I feel that somehow the world *ought* to be a far better place? Don't I know, deep down, that there is high beauty and joy out there somewhere?'

There is the secular doubt about meaning and hope: 'Is it really true that eventually everything I do (and everyone has ever done) will be extinguished in the death of the solar system? So that ultimately it makes no difference whether I live a good or cruel life? How do I avoid a sense of radical insignificance? Don't I know, deep down, that I *am* here for a purpose?'

So, paradoxically, we live in an age in which both believers and non-believers in God struggle with doubts about their basic beliefs about life and the nature of the universe.

Most books written by Christian authors addressing this contemporary situation look only at the problems that Christian believers face. They answer the doubts that challenge believers. Such books are important and I wrote one of them myself! There is, however, a great dearth of books that honestly and practically address the doubts and difficulties that secular, 'no religious preference' people face.

Charles Taylor himself, in his magisterial *A Secular Age,* takes this path. He knows the problems of those who follow the secular way and he respectfully points them out. But his work is scholarly and therefore inaccessible to most readers. The same is true of a number of other thinkers who, over the past thirty years, have begun to recognize these secular doubts and difficulties. We need books, then, that not only listen to the everyday experiences and problems of modern people, but that also draw on the best recent scholarship as well as ancient biblical wisdom in order to address these issues in an understanding, accessible, but challenging way.

Pete Nicholas has written such a book. He uses both his academic training and his pastoral experience to address the deeply felt tensions that affect young people in secular society today. While evidencing the breadth of his background reading, he writes in an easy-to-read and practical way that sympathetically helps readers to think through and wrestle with the perennial, unavoidable Big Issues of human life – truth, morality, happiness, identity, hope – and shows a way forward for all who are struggling.

I could not be more encouraged by Pete's book. We need an entire movement of writers and thinkers who, like Pete, can distil the wisdom of the far past and also of the more recent work of phil-osophers, theologians and social scientists, to help people navigate the cross-currents of our secular age. If you are looking for someone to help you address the unprecedented challenges people face today to find community, a meaning that suffering can't take away, a hope that endures lifelong, and a secure and resilient identity – start here.

Tim Keller

As a society we find ourselves with a dull ache of regret, looking around for something that we need but can no longer find.

Introduction

A place for God

Marie Kondo, the Japanese 'organizing consultant', is a guru for decluttering your life and she is big business, particularly now in the West. It makes sense that, with the excesses of consumerism, we might need someone to help us deal with all the clutter we accumulate. I myself have an affinity with the desire to tidy up and rationalize. My wife, Rebecca, and I often joke that she is a 'leaver' and I am a 'putter'; she leaves things around the house in 'useful' places and I follow behind, obsessively putting them away! And, though we joke about it, a few years ago my desire for decluttering led to the loss of something precious.

Our first son, Oliver, had recently been born and baptized. His birth was particularly special because getting pregnant hadn't been straightforward for us. Friends and family had kindly sent us congratulations cards, each of which had a special poignance given the wait for Oliver's arrival. However, in a desire to 'tidy up' one day, I threw the cards out. Rebecca came home, immediately noticed they were missing and asked me what I had done with them. Realizing my stupidity, I ran out to the communal recycling bin. It was too late: just an hour or so before, the recycling collection had taken place; the bin was empty and the cards were gone. Fortunately, my wife is very forgiving, but she was obviously upset. So was I. I had thrown the cards out thinking we didn't want or need them any more. Ever since then I have regularly found myself regretting my folly and wishing I could get them back. More recently, I have found myself wondering whether culturally we are experiencing something similar.

There has been a fair bit of decluttering and throwing out in the realm of ideas, sparked by the period in history that we call the Enlightenment (from the mid seventeenth century onwards). As with any desire for rationalization, it has been a case of getting rid of ideas and beliefs that we no longer feel we need or want, to make space for other things that we do. Superstition has given way to reason. Religion has given way to science. Uniformity has given way to pluralism. Astrology has given way to astronomy, and so on.

Much of this change has been good and important. I think, however, that in some key areas we have thrown out too much and, as with the example of my folly, we are feeling the loss. As a society we find ourselves with a dull ache of regret, looking around for something that we need but can no longer find.

Diagnosing the problem

If you walked in for a medical appointment, the doctor wouldn't blindly guess at a diagnosis; he or she would look at the symptoms to help identify the problem and propose a treatment. The symptoms caused by what we have lost are all around us, but for now let me identify three aspects that I know I have felt in my own life, and I imagine many of you have as well: restlessness, psychological strain and a culture of fear.

First of all, restlessness. Pretty much anyone you ask will tell you that we are busier today than we have ever been. Think of how often you answer the question, 'How are you?' with the answer, 'A bit too busy.' Think of the numerous reports on the increasing levels of stress. In 2018, 74% of people in the UK said they felt 'overwhelmed or unable to cope' and those levels were higher in the younger generations, with 83% of 18–24-year-olds reporting feeling that way.[1] And yet the strange fact is that we *aren't* busier today than we have ever been. The data just doesn't bear it out. The average working week in the

2

West was sixty hours at the end of the nineteenth century and now it is nearly half that, thirty-three hours.[2] And it is not just paid economic work that is decreasing; with ever more labour-saving devices, things such as housework take less time too. Therefore, if we work less than before and have such investment in our rest, why are we so 'rest-less'? Tiredness may be able to be fixed by a good night's sleep but restlessness points to our inner life: it's a symptom of the state of our soul.

Second, psychological strain. There is no doubt now that mental illness is on the rise across the West and it can't be explained by alleged 'under-reporting' in previous generations. For quite some time (at least as far back as the 1930s), researchers have been comparing the incidence of mental illness across generations and these studies show that levels of anxiety and depression are significantly higher than previously and are higher among younger members of our society.[3] Add to that the rising rates of addiction across society and the increasing number of things people are becoming addicted to, from shopping to gaming, from pornography to food, and something is clearly very wrong.

Trying to figure out what factors are driving these trends is complex, and of course every case will have its particularities to that person. When considering the wider phenomenon described, however, we do need to consider broader social factors that may be causing it. As one commentator has asked, 'What greater indictment of a system could there be than an epidemic of mental illness?'[4]

Third, a culture of fear. The opposite of security is fear and, as noted by the sociologist Barry Glassner, we have a 'culture of fear'.[5] Glassner reports three out of four Americans feeling more afraid than they did two decades ago and, in a corresponding book focused on Europe, Heinz Bude comments:

In its substance, too, fear is infinite: fear of school, fear of heights, fear of poverty, fear of heart disease, fear of terrorism, fear of losing social status, fear of commitment, fear of inflation.[6]

Yet both writers argue that the fears are unfounded:

Why are so many fears in the air, and so many of them unfounded? Why, as crime rates plunged throughout the 1990s did two-thirds of Americans believe they were soaring? . . . In the late 1990s the number of drug users had decreased by half compared to a decade earlier . . . So why did a majority of adults rank drug abuse as the greatest danger to America's youth? . . . Give us a happy ending and we write a new disaster story.[7]

And it goes on: health fears when life expectancy in the West is as high as it has ever been; fear of terrorist attacks amidst a generation that thankfully hasn't known a major war and mass conscription; fear of foreigners 'taking our jobs' when in the UK employment is at its highest since 1975 . . . the fears multiply.[8]

None of this is to suggest that there aren't any things to be afraid of. Instead, it is to say that the level of fear is disproportionate to the general level of threat. Consider, for example, this analysis of the recent coronavirus crisis from Lord Sumption, a justice in the UK Supreme Court, and an author and historian writing in the midst of the epidemic:

Fear is dangerous. It is the enemy of reason. It suppresses balance and judgment. And it is infectious. . . . Is the coronavirus the latest and most damaging example? Epidemics are not new. Bubonic plague, smallpox, cholera, typhoid, meningitis, Spanish flu all took a heavy toll in their time. An earlier generation would not have understood the current hysteria over COVID-19, whose symptoms are milder and whose case mortality is lower than any of these. What has changed? For one thing, we have become much more risk-averse. We no longer accept the wheel of fortune. We take security for granted. We do not tolerate tragedies.[9]

If you met someone who perpetually suffered from debilitating fear, beyond what is reasonable or normal, what would you conclude? Wouldn't you be concerned? Wouldn't you wonder whether behind the fear lies a deep-seated insecurity? So what should we conclude about our culture?

Putting these three aspects together – restlessness, psychological ill health and a culture of fear – I wonder if you agree that something is clearly wrong. The examples I have given are not exhaustive, and they aren't intended to be. Numerous social commentators have made similar diagnoses from other related symptoms: polarized and uncivil public discourse, identity politics, racism and the growth of the extreme right and extreme left, the breakdown of community, the erosion of ethical standards and basic morality, increasingly self-oriented materialism, the widening inequalities in the economy . . . I could go on, and I imagine that so could you.

The problems we face are not merely circumstantial, though no doubt circumstances expose them. They are not just confined to a certain demographic within society, though no doubt certain groups feel them more acutely. With these problems bubbling under the surface, it is clear that all is not well. However, as with all diagnoses, there is a danger that we can get preoccupied with the symptoms and miss the root cause. This restless, fearful sense of being ill at ease that pervades much of Western consciousness points us to a deeper problem, a deeper loss that we are struggling to come to terms with.

What have we lost?

Given the title of the book, my diagnosis might not surprise you. I think our main problem is that we have lost God, or, to be more concrete, we have thrown away living with God as a central reality in our lives. After all, if God is God, then he is probably not that easily 'lost'. Equally, I do not just think that we have lost a general idea of 'god', but that, in our desire to declutter and make way for new ideas, we have largely jettisoned the Christian God who has been central to so much of Western society and our perception of the world, ourselves and how we should live.

The poet Matthew Arnold memorably wrote:

> The Sea of Faith
> Was once, too, at the full, and round earth's shore
> Lay like the folds of a bright girdle furled.
> But now I only hear
> Its melancholy, long, withdrawing roar,
> Retreating, to the breath
> Of the night-wind, down the vast edges drear
> And naked shingles of the world.[10]

The imagery is poignant. 'A bright girdle [belt]' was once 'furled [wrapped]' around the earth but now the 'vast edges' of the world are grey and exposed to the elements; 'naked'.

The metaphor of the bright belt wrapped around the earth is helpful because it speaks to the way that God is not just a piece of the wider puzzle to be slotted back in, but rather he is the uniting theme of everything, a thread running through all that is and all that we can know, linking everything together and bringing coherence and light.

Christians have sometimes been accused of proposing a 'God of the gaps', as if God is there to fill in the blanks that we can't understand. According to this argument, as human knowledge advances through science and reason, these gaps are filled in and the need for God diminishes. That is an interesting hypothesis, but it is certainly not the kind of God revealed in the Christian Scriptures. As 'the Alpha and the Omega' (Revelation 22:13), he is the God who is 'all in all' (1 Corinthians 15:28). He is depicted in the Bible as uniting everything, binding it together, as if nothing truly makes sense without him and everything ultimately comes from him. Little wonder, then, that if we have lost *this* God, we would be feeling the effects widely and deeply.

Rebuilding our foundations

Today there is an admirable desire to engage in the 'Big Questions of Life'. You can see it in the enormous success of platforms such as TED Talks and the proliferation of related books and online content. As part of my research for this book, I asked some questions of 442 Christian leaders in various spheres of life who come from the Millennial generation.[11] Assuming that they were accurately representing their opinions, when I enquired about the key questions their non-Christian friends were asking, it was notable how these 'big questions' showed up time and again.

- 'Where can I find happiness?' 46.6% were asking this question.
- 'How can I reconcile science with religion?' 41.9%
- 'Can there be real justice?' 33.5%
- 'Where do I belong?' 32.8%
- 'Who can I trust?' 21.3%

With the exception of the question about the compatibility of science with religion, which is a particularly important one for the

West today, these questions aren't new. Traditionally, every society has cohered around a common set of answers to them. Indeed, a large part of what defines one culture over against another is the way these answers are framed and worked out. They form the 'idea' level, otherwise known as the 'metaphysical' level – the foundations that underpin every culture. For any society, having a degree of consensus on these questions gives a sense of stability and coherence. I am suggesting that the reason we feel destabilized today – restless, under strain and fearful – is that these foundations have been eroded. And that in jettisoning God from our beliefs, the central idea that held these foundations together in the West for hundreds of years has been removed and the resulting cracks are getting wider and deeper.

This is why there is such a keen interest in engaging with these issues today. We intuitively know that we need these foundations if we are to flourish individually and as a society, and so we are searching for answers. As someone who has studied for degrees in philosophy, applied sociology and religion, I have spent a lot of my adult life grappling with them and speaking and writing about them. And yet these questions are not confined to the area of academia. If we are to rediscover the stability and coherence that enable us to flourish in life, then we need to start grappling with these questions again rather than accepting that there are no fixed answers to find. With this in mind, these questions will form the core chapters of this book.

Seeking what we have lost

My father-in-law is an architect. He tells me that London is the most difficult and expensive place to build in on earth. Largely, it is to do with the challenges of laying good foundations. Tunnels for the Tube, Victorian sewers, strange bedrock (particularly around the Thames) and even a series of tunnels that only get used by the Royal Mail all provide challenges to laying the foundations that are needed to build. Where I live, near City Road – that iconic thoroughfare that runs through central London – there has been an explosion of high-rises in just the last few years, brought on by recent advances in the technology of laying foundations. What always surprises me is that the foundation stage of the build seems to take the longest. For months the hoardings are up around the site and there is a lot of noise but no sign of any progress. Then, seemingly in a much shorter length of time, the buildings spring up.

Similarly, part of what we have started to do – and what we will continue to do if you will join me on this journey – is to drill down and excavate our own foundational beliefs so that we can re-lay them and build. If the analysis above has been a little unsettling, you may well be seeking to avoid it. 'Are we really restless and fearful? Surely describing the West as having something deeply wrong with it is a bit over the top? Are we *really* building without foundations?' It is said that 'the hardest thing to give is in', and as human beings we do tend to resist the facts when they are challenging. This process is never particularly comfortable, but ask any architect and they will tell you it is essential.

I am aware that a majority of people in the West will respond to my proposition that we need to put God back at the centre of our lives with a number of objections. To be candid, I had many of these objections myself when, as an adult who wasn't a Christian, aged twenty, I first seriously engaged with Christianity. I was fortunate to have good friends who were patient enough to stick with me as I read, discussed and grappled with my objections and the many related questions that were thrown up. Part of my endeavour, therefore, over the coming chapters, will be to seek to deal with a number of these common objections as we explore the wider issues to which they are related:

- Hasn't science disproved Christianity or at least rendered it redundant? (We shall be looking at this question in chapter 1, 'Origins'.)
- Is the Bible credible? Isn't claiming to have 'the truth about God' exclusive and arrogant? (Chapter 2, 'Truth'.)
- Why do we need God to tell us what is right and wrong? (Chapter 3, 'Morality'.)
- Isn't Christianity excessively restrictive and therefore doesn't it deprive us of happiness? (Chapter 4, 'Happiness'.)
- Isn't Christianity repressive and an affront to my personal autonomy? (Chapter 5, 'Identity'.)
- Aren't the claims about Jesus part of a myth, made up and ultimately unbelievable for us today? (Chapter 6, 'Hope'.)

We should always welcome questions. There is an important premise underpinning freedom of speech: if something is true, it will stand up to scrutiny, and if it isn't then isn't it beneficial to show it to be false? That being said, you will know as well as I do that there is a form of questioning that is constructive, coming from a place of curiosity and a genuine desire for engagement. In contrast, there is a type of questioning that is blinkered and destructive, merely seeking to confirm an existing bias. One of the few things I would ask of you as you read on is that you seek to adopt the constructive mode of curiosity and engagement as we explore together what we may have lost.

Three of Jesus' most enduring parables are the parables of the Lost Sheep, the Lost Coin and the Lost (or Prodigal) Son (you can find them in Luke's Gospel, chapter 15). In all three parables that which was lost – a sheep, a coin and a son – are found again and restored.

In all three there is great joy at the restoration. Ultimately that is my hope for all of us, that by engaging with these big questions, examining our foundations and rebuilding where necessary, we will rediscover the vital place God occupies in the world and this will lead to much joy and a restoration of our society.

The stories we tell really matter; they shape how we see ourselves, how we see others and how we see the world.

1

Origins

Where have we come from?

Where have we come from?

'Where are you from?' It used to be a very common question, but in today's globalized world it is not that easy to answer it simply. Author Amanda Mukwashi notes how, as a member of a visible ethnic group, when she replies, 'The UK', the question is often followed by 'But where are you *really* from?'[1] Is the question asking where someone was born? Is it asking about their ethnicity? Is it asking about where they live? Because rarely today are all three of these areas aligned. Nonetheless, being able to answer the question is vital for every person because origins matter.

One of my good friends is Martin Nangoli. In many regards, we are unlikely friends. He grew up in a small village in rural Uganda, ran away from home as a child, lived as a street child for some years and then by God's grace turned his life around and now runs an NGO in Eastern Uganda. My background, life experience, education and opportunities are all very different from his, but it is a joy to call him my friend and I have learned a lot from him. I remember one of the first times that I went with Martin to a meeting in Uganda and we were asked to introduce ourselves. I said, 'Hi, I'm Pete Nicholas and I come from London.' Martin then gave his introduction and it went on for several minutes! It resembled a mixture of a kind of genealogy followed by a summary of his life story:

I am Nangoli Martin, son of Pastor Samueli who is married to Enida, also brother of Moses and . . . from Kikobero village . . . as a small child I ran away from the village . . .

As we became friends I asked Martin why Ugandans often give such long introductions when they meet one another. He replied:

It is only if we know where we are from, and something of our story, that we really get to know one another and work out where we are going.

How true that is. The issue of origins affects the decisions we make, it informs our identity, it shapes where we are going and it determines how we see the world and how we see ourselves. This is why it is so important and why it is a good starting point as we seek to build our foundations.

'Where are *you from*?' has two areas of focus. The word 'from?' nods to context, with the 'you' pointing to who you are and what you are like. So to understand our origins we will first consider our context, the universe we live in and how we understand it, before we turn to thinking about who we are as human beings. Along the way we will need to grapple with the important issue of science and religion and their compatibility.

Our context: cosmos and space

On Monday 26 November 2018 NASA's Mars InSight probe touched down on the red planet. It was a wonderful technological achieve-ment and I mean that literally: it was something that should inspire wonder.

But what was noticeable in the news reports at the time was the lack of excitement generated by the event. Sure, there were the now-expected photos of the NASA scientists awkwardly high-fiving as the probe landed, but then the news quickly faded into the background. Even the name of the probe was markedly less interesting than other missions. Early NASA flights were characterized by the names of mythical gods, such as 'Mercury' and 'Apollo', but more recently we are into catchy and not very inspiring acronyms: 'Interior Exploration using Seismic Investigations, Geodesy and Heat Transport'; hence InSight. It hardly inspires.

Yes, the name does what it says on the tin, but this is the pinnacle of exploration, our 'final frontier'. Shouldn't there be a greater sense of marvel and awe? Even one of the British scientists working on the mission seemed to find it all a bit mundane: 'Where we land is an intentionally dull place,' said Neil Bowles, a planetary scientist at Oxford University who was involved in the mission; 'it's flat, empty and hopefully not very windy. And that is precisely what we need.'[2]

If all this seems a bit far away from your lived experience, then please reflect on how you felt the last time you got a new gadget (iPhone, Android, computer). How excited were you when you got it? How quickly did the excitement and happiness, if indeed there was any, wear off? Or think about a bit of countryside you are familiar with. Was there a time when you first saw it when it captivated you? The colour and hue of hills, light glinting off water, clouds rolling down a valley. But after a time it can become all too familiar, even mundane.

The Christian thinker and writer G. K. Chesterton once wrote, 'The world will never starve for want of wonders, but for want of wonder.'[3]

In the medieval era and for the ancients the universe was seen as a 'cosmos'. It was an arena tingling with life, more like a festival of dance than an impersonal machine. Planets were called 'heavenly bodies', which made music that governed their movements in the night sky. As humans we were like children peering in at the window of a great mansion, trying to get a glimpse of the things inside, things wonderful and awe-inspiring, sometimes things scary and un-controllable. Theirs was an enchanted universe.

Today there is a tragic irony in the fact that scientific advancement has enabled us to explore and understand our universe better than ever before, but rather than this inducing wonder, we have actually lost our sense of wonder. Our universe is mostly made up of 'space'. The word shift from 'cosmos' to 'space' is significant. Space implies emptiness, nothingness. As the 2012 Facebook advert celebrating 1 billion users stated, 'The universe, it is vast and dark, and makes us wonder if we are alone.'[4]

Implicitly we have been told that this trade-off between the wonderful and the scientific is inevitable. It is a bit like the difference between children reading fairy stories and adults reading the news. One may be more interesting and may capture the imagination, but it is just fantasy. What we 'grown-ups' need to deal with are facts, like the bore Thomas Gradgrind in Charles Dickens's *Hard Times*, a man who goes around

> with a rule and a pair of scales, and the multiplication table always in his pocket, sir, ready to weigh and measure any parcel of human nature, and tell you exactly what it comes to. It is a mere question of figures, a case of simple arithmetic.[5]

But what if this is a false dichotomy? What if this buffer (as phil-osopher Charles Taylor has called it[6]) that we have erected around our scientific and modern selves, keeping out the fantastic and the enchanted, is depriving us of a world view that is no less scientific and grown-up, but one which instead of removing wonder, cultivates it and promotes it?

Science and religion, not science versus religion

Even if you haven't read Mary Shelley's *Frankenstein*, you may know that the real monster in the book is not the creature, but Victor Frankenstein himself. Victor is a brilliant scientist who one day does the miraculous and creates life. He does it not because he should but just because he can. But he doesn't give any thought to how to govern his creation or the impact that his moral flaws will have on such a powerful creature. Victor's neglect of his creature ends up in tragedy. His creation becomes a monster, who ends up killing and destroying much that is dear to Victor.[7]

Part of the reason this story has endured is that the lessons it teaches are timeless. The danger of creating something that is more powerful than we can properly govern. Doing something just because we can without first asking whether we *should*. The way that as human beings our character failings leave an indelible impression on our innovations and corrupt them, causing us great harm. These warnings resonate in the modern scientific movement. And then there is the supreme warning of a creation becoming so distorted that it tries to kill off its creator. So, has science killed God?

Some scientists claim that by their scientific endeavour they have killed off any need for God. 'God is dead; now we have science!' This is despite the origins of the modern scientific movement being rooted in the Judeo-Christian world view, and despite there being no inherent contradiction between science and Christianity. Here is Frankenstein's creature corrupted and wreaking havoc on its originators.

The eminent historian A. N. Whitehead was interested in tracing the roots of modern science. He compared the prevailing medieval culture and its belief in Christianity with other cultures and observed:

When we compare this [scientific] tone of thought in Europe with the attitude of other civilisations when left to themselves, there seems but one source for its origin. It must come from the medieval insistence on the rationality of God, conceived as with the personal energy of Jehovah ... Every detail was supervised and ordered: the search into nature could only result in the vindication of the faith in rationality.[8]

He is saying that modern science has at its very core a presupposition of the orderliness and rationality of the world. It is predicated on certain basic assumptions and these assumptions originate from a culture deeply shaped by a Judeo-Christian world view in which there is a belief in a rational and orderly world because of a belief in a rational and orderly God who made it and sustains it.

Please note that A. N. Whitehead is not saying that science didn't *also* arise in other non-Christian cultures; it clearly did. But this causes us to ask what accounted for the explosion in modern science whereby the West rapidly outstripped the rest of the world in its technological advancement and scientific thinking. What was the seedbed for this rapid growth that has so profoundly shaped Western culture? Far from its being a reaction against God, historically it originated from a belief in God.

For the atheist who claims that it is 'science versus religion', this much should make them pause for thought. If the two are in fact so incompatible, why did Christianity provide such a fruitful context for the modern scientific movement to grow and thrive in? Equally, why do so many eminent scientists, including multiple winners of Nobel Prizes for Physics, Chemistry and Physiology and Medicine, describe themselves as Christians? Have they somehow missed the inherent contradiction in their position, or *is* there no contradiction?[9]

In fact, in the UK only a minority (32%) of all scientists themselves think religion and science are in conflict.[10]

I would suggest that the very framing of the 'science versus religion' debate has been determined by a vocal minority who hold not just to 'science' but to a belief in what is sometimes called 'scientism'. Science is the study of the natural order and how it is organized and structured. It is one area of study and one area of human life among many, along with aesthetics, morality, politics, etc. Scientism is very different; it seeks to be a 'grand theory of everything'. It claims that science can explain all things (and, ironically, claims this with an almost religious fervour). Scientism boldly says that the scientific method can and should underpin all areas of human life and study and is sufficient to account for all areas of human existence and thinking. Careful reflection shows us that it is not science vs. God but scientism vs. God.

But, when you think about this, isn't the scientism claim very odd and something of an overreach? First, isn't it a wildly inaccurate description of reality? Can you think of anyone, let alone the vocal proponents of scientism themselves, such as the 'New Atheists', who makes important value-based decisions such as whom they should marry, how they should bring up their children, which house they want to buy and live in, *only* on the basis of science and the scientific method? Science may play some limited role in some of those decisions (the survey of the house, for example), but it plays no part in how we feel about a house, or whom we love, or why we want children to share their toys rather than hog them. Second, isn't the claim that science *alone* can determine religion and morality also an obvious overreach? Albert Einstein shrewdly dismissed both the idea that religious belief could be reduced from science and the assertion, which was popular in his day as in ours, that science has nothing to do with religion. He thought that 'both attitudes . . . display a very superficial concept of science and also of religion'. He went on to say in the same discussion: 'You are right in speaking of the moral foundations of science, but you cannot turn round and speak of the scientific foundations of morality . . . every attempt to reduce ethics to scientific formulae must fail.'[11]

One of the reasons why the set-up of science versus Christianity is wrong is that science and religion are dealing with very different questions. Science deals with mechanisms and 'how stuff works' (to put it simply), morality deals with purpose and 'how life *should* be lived' and religion deals with authorship and the question of 'who created life'. These areas may mutually inform one another, but we all understand that they are distinct. That's why they are classified into different sections in our libraries! To play them off against one another is like saying that because you understand some of the coding in the operating system of an iPhone (mechanism), this means that you don't need any guidance on why you shouldn't become addicted to a gambling app (morality) and, further, that you can't believe that Steve Jobs ever existed (authorship). This is what philosophers rightly call a category error: confusing the distinct categories and what they can and can't tell us. Hardly a very scientific mistake to make.

A scientific *and* wonderful world view

So, if science is not opposed to religion in general and Christianity in particular, what would it look like to have an integrated view of the world rather than to buy into a strange false dichotomy? In the medieval cosmos, technology (yes, they did have it then!) helped them to pull back the curtain and gaze more intently on the glory within. Despite some pitting of science against religion in the centuries that followed, most held the integrated view. That is why Psalm 111:2 was carved above the first Cavendish Physics Laboratory in Cambridge University in 1874: 'The works of the LORD are great, sought out of all them that have pleasure therein' (KJV). Religion was a powerful motive propelling scientific endeavour. If the world was inherently good, and God was glorious, then these were important motivations for exploring it, mining its depths and searching out its secrets. If God has given us the gift of creation, and to innovate is something that is 'godlike' because he is the great Creator, then these are compelling reasons for being inventive and curious. It was not that our ancestors were unscientific, far from it: science had the role of discovery in order to induce wonder. Today, technology often has a different function: to explore – but to what end? As the Facebook advert I mentioned earlier put it, 'Maybe the reason we make all of these things is to remind ourselves that we are not [alone]'.

My wife and I love watching the BBC's *Planet Earth* TV series narrated by Sir David Attenborough. The quality of the photography is stunning, but of course the stars of the show are not the photographers or videographers, gifted as they are; they are just there to bring home to us how stunning our planet is. Sir David's commentary serves a similar function as he talks about the 'miracle of life' or the 'glorious' display of a bird. But reflect for a moment on the language being used. 'Miracle' and 'glorious' are words originating from the religious sphere. Does it not strike you as odd that so often when he, a vocal atheist, is reaching for the hyperbole to capture the marvel of what he is witnessing, he uses such overtly religious and super-natural words? I'm not at all suggesting that he has no right to do so (I am glad he does), but isn't it telling that in those moments where we are awestruck (again, notice the phrase), the secular world view just seems bereft of the resources to describe adequately what we see and feel? Science on its own may be part of the explanation. Yes, a bird-of-paradise dancing in its courtship spectacle is trying to secure a mate to further its gene pool, but is that really a sufficient account on its own? Isn't the magisterial beauty of its display, the glint of the feathers, the carnival of colour, something more? If we see science as stemming from and reinforced by Christianity, rather than at odds with it, then we can give voice to these vital inclinations not just as a rhetorical flourish but as an integrated and essential part of a world that is no less scientific but no less glorious and wonderful. Isn't that the way we intuitively want to see the world?

We have forgotten what we are

Having looked at our context, the cosmos in which we live, let's now look in the mirror and consider the nature of humanity; where are *you* from? 'I understand the cause of your sickness. You have forgotten what you are.' So says Lady Philosophy to the grieving Boethius in *The Consolation of Philosophy*.[12] The words she spoke to Boethius in the darkness of his prison cell resonate with us today. Has forgetting who we are caused a kind of sickness?

One of the recent rediscoveries in Western society is the importance of narrative. The stories we tell really matter; they shape how we see ourselves, how we see others and how we see the world. Unfortunately, although we have rediscovered the power of narrative, post-modernity tells us that these stories can't really be true because there is no such thing as true or false (we'll come to this in the next chapter). As a result, there is a carelessness about the narratives we tell one another. But stories do matter, and whether or not they are true also matters.

When it comes to humanity we seem to want to hold two competing stories in tension. One story is the secular naturalistic story, and it's not very uplifting. Here is evolutionary biologist and author Richard Dawkins's take on the story:

> The universe we observe has precisely the properties we should expect if there is, at bottom, no design, no purpose, no evil and no good, nothing but blind, pitiless indifference. As that

unhappy poet A.E. Housman put it: 'For Nature, heartless, witless Nature Will neither care nor know.' DNA neither cares nor knows. DNA just is. And we dance to its music.[13]

Whether or not you chime with Dawkins's blunt assessment, it is difficult to disagree with his conclusions *if* his naturalistic starting point is right. If the universe is the result of no design, no ultimate purpose, just blind forces, then surely he's right: DNA doesn't care. We are just atoms thrown together, we are not objectively any more special than a frog or a tree stump, and there is no ultimate purpose for our lives or any real value to us. As Heinrich Himmler chillingly wrote, 'There is nothing particular about man. He is but a part of this world.'[14]

But alongside this we also seem to want to hold another story. This is the story that is written on a thousand billboards, shared in texts between friends when they try to pick one another up from life's difficulties, and infuses the lyrics of our songs: 'You are special'; 'Because you're worth it'; 'You are beautiful no matter what they say'; 'You can do anything, achieve anything you set your mind to'. I hope you can see just how much these two stories are in tension. The naturalistic story denigrates humanity; this second one almost deifies humanity.

Could it be that some of the symptoms we identified in the introduction – restlessness, psychological strain and a culture of fear – are caused by trying to hold in tension these competing stories about what we are? Living with such a strong contradictory pull on our identity can't be easy. I remember talking to a young man some years back who said to me:

The problem is our culture tells us that we are nothing and yet we can be everything and I think the tension puts such a pressure on us because if we don't make it then it's all on us and we just fall back into the abyss.

I wonder, do you identify with this?

Homo sapiens or *imago Dei*?

Our stories about our identity are in tension; as a society, we want to hold to certain core implications about humanity while at the same time getting rid of the religious framework they came from. We hold dearly to the idea of the equality and dignity of all people regardless of ethnicity, gender or social status. We passionately proclaim our human rights. We care deeply about the liberty of minority groups and the oppressed. But where have such beliefs come from? Would it surprise you to know that they have come from Christianity? Would it surprise you to know that even the concept of 'humanism', which is so often pitted against Christianity, arose from Christianity itself?[15]

In Congress on 4 July 1776 the unanimous Declaration of the thirteen United States of America was:

> We hold these truths to be self-evident, that all men are created equal, that they are endowed by their Creator with certain unalienable rights, that among these are life, liberty and the pursuit of happiness.

Do you notice how the foundational beliefs about humanity in this seminal declaration were framed in the context of a Christian world view, in relation to a Creator who endows us with this dignity and equality and therefore our rights? Today we have lifted the humanist values from the statement 'that all men [people] are created equal . . . with certain unalienable rights' but we no longer mention the framework within which they are situated, as if the one can survive without the other. This is a worrying move, though, because the narrative that frames these beliefs really matters. This is the philosophical equivalent of taking a prized golden carp out of a fish pond and expecting it to be OK. Instead, it flaps about in panic, gasping for air, and it won't last long unless it is put back in its original context. Or, to think of it another way, as philosopher Alasdair MacIntyre argues in his book *After Virtue*, 'I can only answer the question "What am I to do?" if I can answer the prior question "Of what story or stories do I find myself a part?"'[16] Therefore, if we forget or stop narrating the story, it won't be long before we lose the ethics that were attached to that story altogether.

Homo sapiens means 'wise man' or 'wise person'. But I hope you can see that it is not a wise move to divorce an understanding of ourselves from the framework that gave life to our foundational views about humanity in the first place.

And it's not just our basic human rights and the equality of all people that have come from the Christian world view. The starting point of Scripture's view of humanity that we are *imago Dei* (the image of God; Genesis 1:27) flows out in a myriad of life-giving streams:

- The intrinsic worth of every human being and the sanctity of life not predicated on age, status, achievements, ability or disability, or ethnicity but purely because every person is made by God and reflects his image, and is therefore of inestimable worth.
- The priority of relationships and love (over, for example, material possessions) because we are God's image and God is a God who is, within himself as Trinity, love.
- The responsibility of those vested with power to help the weak and vulnerable because God, the strongest being in the

universe, is humanity's great helper (Deuteronomy 33:29) and the helper of the vulnerable (Psalm 113:7).

- The importance of education for children (which in the UK can be traced back to the Christian social reformer Lord Shaftesbury), because all people are made in the image of God and the image of a thinking and speaking God.[17]
- The inherent freedom of every person because God's people are a redeemed and liberated people (Exodus 20:1–2), which gave rise to the abolition of slavery, initiated in the West by the Christian William Wilberforce.
- The intrinsic right that a woman has over her own body in a relationship with a man, first articulated in 1 Corinthians 7:3–5 (note the way the Apostle Paul assumes a woman is able to say 'no' to her husband – a radical view at the time and for hundreds of years subsequently).

These and many more foundational Western beliefs about humanity all originate from a Christian world view and particularly from a self-understanding as *imago Dei*. As C. S. Lewis wrote:

> There are no ordinary people . . . Every person we have ever looked upon, smiled at, frowned at, greeted, encouraged, insulted, slandered, touched is a person bearing the marks of divine likeness and the Imago Dei.[18]

So where are you from?

I have two young children, Oliver and Tobi. They are simultaneously exhausting and enlivening. Exhausting because their appetite for joy seems insatiable; enlivening for the same reason. They love it when I pick them up and throw them in the air and catch them. They squeal with laughter. 'More, Daddy. Again!' I do it again. 'Again! Again!' And so it goes on. I don't think I can remember a time when they have asked me to stop before I have become tired. It is marvellous that something as trivial as being thrown up in the air can induce so much joy in children. How different things are when we grow up. Whereas a child seems to find joy and excitement around every corner, can you even remember the last time you felt that way? How rare it is. What has changed to drain us of our joy? The world is the same place that delights our children. It is we who have changed.

The paradox of the late modern world in which we live is that we have more reason than ever before to experience joy, but it seems to be more elusive than ever. Again, *we* have changed. Our view of the universe and our view of ourselves have deprived us of the wonder we once had. As a society we may have told ourselves that this is an inevitable part of growing up, but I don't buy it. Realism need not lead to cynicism if we have the right view of what is 'real'. And what could be more wonderful of all than if God were real? With God back in place in our lives, space would become the cosmos and *homo sapiens* would become the *imago Dei*. With God back in place, science would become a means of inducing awe in a glorious world made by an even more glorious Creator. With God back in place, we would know the reason for the many human rights we cherish and we would know the one who endows us with those rights. With God back in place, the normal would become the wonderful and the everyday would become the miraculous as we rediscover our origins and start to rebuild our foundations from this starting point.

The question of truth underpins every other question.

2
Truth

What is true and where is truth found?

Post-truth

I have a friend, a GP, who told me a story that seems to sum up our culture's view of truth. It was about a consultation she had with a teenager (appropriately anonymous) in which the young woman came in and showed her a new tattoo that had got infected, a small symbol on her hip. 'Please don't tell my parents,' she said anxiously to the GP; 'they don't know I've got a tattoo and they'd kill me if they found out.' My friend reassured her about doctor–patient confidentiality and then asked, 'Out of interest, what does the symbol mean?' 'Oh, it's a value that's very important to me,' said the young woman. 'It's the Japanese symbol for truth!'

Truth. On the one hand we want it because we recognize that it is a good and vital thing, but on the other hand being a truthful person is somewhat challenging. To reflect on how vital truth is, consider why fake news is such big news. We hate the idea that we are being lied to. Or why are the most highly regarded values among Millennials (those born between the early 1980s and the early 2000s) authenticity and integrity? These values are all about truth. Authenticity is being true to yourself; integrity is being consistently true to yourself across different spheres of life. Think of the way that over the past few decades there has been a huge growth in the number and profile of public inquiries, all trying to 'get to the truth' of what happened: The Leveson Inquiry into the press, the Grenfell Tower Inquiry, The Iraq Inquiry. Sixty-nine public inquiries were launched between 1990 and 2017, more than three times the nineteen started in the previous thirty years, and we have to look as far back as 1991 for a year when there was no active public inquiry. We are passionate about truth.

On the other hand, we are nervous about truth claims. Whether we realize it or not, we have breathed in the cultural air of the philosopher Michel Foucault, who argued that truth claims are power plays. Therefore, we are sceptical about governments and their claims because many regimes, whether in the past or in the present, manipulate truth as a way of increasing their power. We are wary of the strident rhetoric of religious extremists whose 'truth' seems to bring harm and hurt. Even with those who aren't extremists, we are uncomfortable with what seem to be the arrogant claims of those who say they know the 'truth about God'. We are sceptical about the spin machines of politicians and businesses who claim they have the truth but then seem to edit the facts to advance their own agenda. We yearn for truth but we are sceptical about those who claim to have it.

What this tension between our longing for truth and our nervousness about those who claim to 'have the truth' has led to is not a jettisoning of the desire for truth but a shift in the grounds of truth. The Oxford English Dictionary's (OED) 2016 word of the year was 'post-truth'. The word does not mean 'I am so over truth; all I want is lies!' Instead, the OED defines post-truth as

> relating to or denoting circumstances in which objective facts are less influential in shaping public opinion than appeals to emotion and personal belief.[1]

This means that now when we want to assess the truth about something or someone, how we feel is more significant than external facts. As a result, it is increasingly common to hear people talking about 'what is true for me' and each person, individually, is seen as an arbiter of truth. But as we have made this move, large cracks have started to emerge.

The rise of fake news. The resurgence of propaganda and foreign powers employing disinformation tactics to influence votes. The adoption of some of these tactics by mainline parties in Western democracies. The big ethical questions we are facing as science becomes more powerful: are questions about eugenics, beginning of life ethics and euthanasia, for example, really just opinions, or is it true that there is objective right and wrong?

Now, I am sure you can see why it is important that we grapple with this question of truth early on in our journey, because it goes right to the heart of what our discussion is really about. As you read this book, is it just a discussion of opinions or are we seeking truth? When we talk about life's big questions, such as how you and I should live, are these moral claims just statements of personal preference (a bit like you may enjoy chocolate ice cream but I like strawberry), or are we seeking to discern an actual true and best way for all people? When I write about God, is he a real being that you may meet or come to know, is it true that he exists, or is 'God' just an interesting idea to muse on, like the question, 'How many angels can you fit on a pinhead?' The question of truth underpins every other question.

A division in truth

Because of our nervousness about those who claim to have the truth, there has been a split down the middle of truth into what is known as the 'fact/value dichotomy'. According to this view, the world is divided into certain areas where we can know the facts – science, mathematics and historical events – and other areas where there is no objective truth but just subjective values and opinions, such as in religion, politics and ethics. This distinction is so pervasive that it goes unnoticed and seems uncontroversial today, but it's actually a unique view largely confined to our modern Western society. Think of the way that people commonly say, 'I am entitled to my opinion,' but as yet I have never heard anyone say, 'I am entitled to my own fact!' That is the fact/value dichotomy at work.

On the face of things, this seems like a good distinction to make. What better way to cool down the infighting among religious groups and politicians than by helping them see that they are not discussing truth but just debating opinions? What better way to help people in a globalized society to get on than recognizing that different individuals and different cultures have different beliefs, ethical standards and values, which aren't true or false, right or wrong; they are just preferences. Meanwhile, in the real world, in areas such as science we can still make truth claims because after all those can be verified as true . . . can't they?

Ultimately, this is seen as part of the problem with, for example, Christians who claim that the Bible is 'true', isn't it? First, haven't they read the post-truth script? We don't believe in truth in the realm of religion any more. Second, don't they recognize that it's a bit arrogant, maybe even dangerous, to claim to know the truth about God? The reason we got rid of truth claims in those areas is that we fear they will stir up trouble and maybe even cause conflict.

Well, while there is lots that is good about this desire for peaceable and constructive communication between different beliefs, I think we are going about it the wrong way. First, because our fact/value dichotomy ultimately breaks down in a number of significant ways and, second, because there is a way to enable civil dialogue that avoids power plays without necessarily jettisoning truth claims.

Why we shouldn't seek to divide truth

First, there is the inherent contradiction of saying, 'All talk of truth in religion or ethics is just opinion and not actually true.' The problem, as philosopher Simon Blackburn has noted, is that when someone makes such a claim they unwittingly 'judo flip' the very claim that they want to make and it becomes self-refuting.[2] So, reflect on how you would answer the question, 'Is it *true* that there is no truth in religion, politics and ethics any more, only opinion?' If you say, 'Yes, that's true', then you yourself are now making an objective truth claim and therefore contradicting your own statement. If you say, 'No, that's not true', then you are also contradicting your statement. This point is not just some clever philosophizing; rather, it exposes how hard it is to say anything without appealing to truth.

If that's left you scratching your head, then, second, the fact/value dichotomy just doesn't function as is claimed, because there isn't in reality a neat division between facts and values. To illustrate this, consider what happens when someone is exposed on social media for making a racist comment. The online community doesn't respond, 'I don't think we can know the truth about that because racism is just a value and there's no truth in that sphere', do they? Instead, everyone starts tweeting, retweeting and posting screenshots of the offending post to find out whether the person truly did make a racist comment. Truth about values such as racism, bigotry and injustice really matters.

Or think about when someone is said to be 'very generous with their money'. Generosity is clearly a value, but who would claim that you can't verify that statement as true? You can look at how they spend their money and what percentage of their income they actually give away, for example. It is verifiable. Similarly, reflect on the value claim that a footballer is very skilful. Skill is a value that can be assessed.

In fact, professional sport is so good at assessing it that we can assign monetary value to it and award footballer of the year prizes!

Therefore, because values can be assessed, philosopher Hilary Putnam argues:

> There are many sorts of statements ... amenable to such terms as 'correct,' 'incorrect,' 'true,' 'false,' 'warranted,' and 'unwarranted' – that are not descriptions [value-free facts], but that are under rational control, governed by standards [factual values] ... Not even David Hume would be willing to classify, for example, 'generous,' 'elegant,' 'skillful,' as concepts [values] to which no 'fact' corresponds.[3]

The fact/value dichotomy just doesn't work.

Third, and most problematical, by shifting into subjectivity and opinions in so many areas we have opened ourselves up to manipulation and fake news. Think of the way that most newspapers are organized. The first part of the paper is the 'news' and then there is the opinion or comment section. The distinction is important: establish the facts about the news and then comment on it. In our post-truth age, however, we are not so interested in the plain facts of what has happened; we prefer comments and opinions, and the more provocative the better. According to Alison Gow, Editor in Chief of Reach plc (one of the UK's biggest news publishers, with more than 240 publications including the *Daily Mirror* and the *Mail on Sunday*), most newspaper website readers today merely scan the headlines and then go to the comments thread without bothering to read the story (the facts).[4] Not only that, but social media algorithms push higher up our news feeds the items that are shared, and the salacious and overstated is shared much more than just boring 'truths'. Put this all together and, as Roy Greenslade, Professor of Journalism at London's City University, commented:

> The lack of a distinction between news and comment has imprinted itself on readers. Now they either cannot distinguish the difference or, just as worryingly, even if they can it would appear they no longer care. Time perhaps to coin a neologism for news-as-comment in the style of the one applied to broadcasting integration of information and entertainment: *infotainment*.[5]

But of course this is much more serious than just a corruption of the news and some politicians getting away with their fake news claims. Because we are no longer as concerned with truth, or perhaps because we no longer seek truth in large areas of our lives, we are losing the ability to discern truth. The political commentator Walter Lippman (1889–1974) wrote, 'There can be no liberty for a community which lacks the means to detect lies.'[6] He was pointing out that truth is bound up with liberty. Trade in truth and you are giving up freedom. This is why Aleksandr Solzhenitsyn, a Nobel Prizewinner for Literature, was wrongfully imprisoned in a labour camp for eleven years under Stalin's Soviet regime because of his writings pointing out the lies and propaganda. He resisted the oppression not by saying 'liberty and justice are just opinions' but by fighting for truth. 'One word of truth', he famously said, quoting an old Russian proverb, 'outweighs the entire world.'

But if we can no longer tell the difference between true and false, or if we no longer really care, then we become easy to manipulate and enslave. It surely can't be a coincidence that recent elections in both the US and the UK have seen disinformation tactics employed by mainstream political parties that would once only be seen behind the Iron Curtain. Sure, some politicians have always had their dirty tricks, but widespread disinformation and propaganda is a hugely concerning paradigm shift that we seem to have just shrugged our shoulders and accepted.

Rethinking the nature of truth

If the fact/value dichotomy has created some big problems in Western society and ultimately doesn't work, I want to suggest that we need to rethink our view of truth.

One of the shifts that occurred during the Enlightenment was that truth became decoupled from God and was attached to humanity as the ultimate arbiter of what is true. No longer was truth revealed by God, but humanity would discover truth independently of God. Partly this was because the church had abused its privileged position, and so arguably it wasn't as much an indictment of God as a rejection of the church. However, the baby got thrown out with the bathwater and God was jettisoned along with the church. What would it look like to rethink truth with God back in place?

The Christian Scriptures teach something surprising about truth, namely that truth is personal. Jesus Christ claims:

> I am the way and the truth and the life. No one comes to the
> Father except through me.
> (John 14:6)

Now, before we deal with the uniqueness claim in the second half of the verse that gets our modern sensibilities so riled up, please notice the first half of the claim. Jesus doesn't claim to bring us truth, or to be the one who can show us where to find truth; he doesn't even claim to be the one who has the truth: he claims to *be* the truth. In other words, he is saying that all truth is bound up with him as a person. Put another way, he is saying that truth is personal and cannot be disconnected from the personal nature of God. So the foundational truths about the universe and our existence are not found in a doctrine or a dogma, or in an equation or a number (like 42 in Douglas Adams's *The Hitchhiker's Guide to the Galaxy*!): they are found in a person, Jesus Christ. What difference does this make?

Jesus' integrity

If you remember the analysis, on one level we want truth today but on the other hand we are nervous about those who make truth claims because it could just be a mask to hide a power grab. Consequently, we have divided facts and values. But when truth is bound up with a person then it is quite different. Persons have an integrity about them (literally, from 'integer', meaning whole). That is, in a person, facts and values come together. If someone espouses their values then you can look at the facts of their life and see if they correspond. Perhaps this is why we are so concerned with authenticity today, because we can intuitively see when a person's life contradicts their lip.

Well, what about Jesus? Jesus claims to be God himself and, because God is love, he espouses the law of love: 'Love your enemies and pray for those who persecute you' (Matthew 5:44, esv). It sounds attractive; a high ideal that would surely improve the world if people could just live this way. What about Jesus' life? Most remarkably of all, Jesus lived this out. He lived an unparalleled life of love, welcoming the outsider, accepting the rejected, breaking down social barriers to include the excluded. Even when he was put to death, having done nothing wrong, he remarkably prayed, 'Father, forgive them, for they do not know what they are doing' (Luke 23:34). Facts and values held together in the beautiful integrity of his person.

I would encourage you not just to take my word for it, but to look at his life as documented in the New Testament and to apply the integrity test yourself. There have been many philosophers and religious gurus down the years who have articulated high ideals, and while Jesus' teaching is unique and uniquely compelling (as we will consider in our chapter on morality), part of what sets him apart is the consistency between his teaching and his life. When, as a young man, I was looking into different philosophers and religious teachers, hoping that they would help me make sense of some of the big questions of life, one of my stubborn complaints was their lack of integrity. Jean-Jacques Rousseau boldly and eloquently argued for 'liberty, equality and fraternity' and his teaching lit the touchpaper that gave rise to the French Revolution. But then he abandoned his own children to an orphanage, lying in his claim that he didn't have the means to raise them. Clearly there was no liberty, fraternity or equality for them. The hypocrisy is chilling. But it is not just Rousseau. As I carefully scrutinized the lives of the world's great thinkers through history, I kept seeing a disconnect between the real and the ideal. Not so with Jesus. His life is carefully documented and his integrity is remarkable.

Jesus' verifiability

But there is more: as a person, Jesus Christ lived in space–time and history. He is not just some abstract idea that someone claims to believe in. He is a person who walked among us and left his indelible mark on the world. As regards truth, this means that he is verifiable. Very often I hear people say things like, 'I wish I had your faith', as though believing in God required a kind of 'Alice in Wonderland' exercise in mental effort:

Alice laughed: 'There's no use trying,' she said; 'one can't believe impossible things.' 'I daresay you haven't had much practice,' said the Queen. 'When I was younger, I always did it for half an hour a day. Why, sometimes I've believed as many as six impossible things before breakfast.'[7]

But I don't believe that the Second World War happened or that Neil Armstrong walked on the moon because I shut my eyes and make myself believe. Nor because those beliefs 'help me get through life'. I believe because the claim corresponds with reality. The facts and the evidence convince me. In fact, even when I don't want to believe something, for example that I was doing 77 mph on a motorway with a 70 mph speed limit, the evidence presented to me (in the form of a photo from the authorities) convinces me. That's how truth works; it is verifiable.

In the same way, Jesus Christ is verifiable as a person and there is ample evidence to engage with. He is the most famous person in world history and the book about him, the Bible, is the most widely circulated and read book in history (and still the most-read book in the world today). This means that there is a huge well of resources to draw on to evaluate what you make of Jesus Christ and whether the claims made about him in Scripture are true.

I remember vividly when I was studying Philosophy, Politics and Economics at university and wasn't a Christian myself the moments when my Christian friends would talk to me about Jesus. I enjoyed the discussions but kept it all at arm's length. One of the things that helped me do that was to say that the Bible had been changed over the years and that, while no credible historian could doubt that there was an influential person called Jesus of Nazareth, the 'historical Jesus' was very different from the person portrayed in the New Testament Gospels. It is quite a well-worn argument. One of my friends then said, 'Pete, if what you say is true then you'll be able to verify it if you look into it. But, as you know, if you were to write a claim like that in one of your university essays, without engaging with the primary source (the Bible), and without giving good evidence to back up your claim, then you'd fail the essay, wouldn't you?' I had to admit they were right. So, as a sceptic, I took them up

39

on the challenge. I thought to myself, 'It will be easy to expose it as untrue.'

I read the Bible for myself, though not all of it at first. I started with Mark's Gospel as one of the historical accounts of Jesus' life. I also read authors who commented on the Bible: some of them were Christians advocating for the Bible's credibility; others were passionate sceptics seeking to discredit it. I wanted to get a balanced view and weigh the evidence. To my shock, the more I read about Jesus, the more Scripture's claims stood up to scrutiny. Eventually, after a number of months of intensely looking into it (when I should have been revising for my finals!), I found myself reluctantly convinced that not only is the New Testament accurate and reliable, but it is vastly more accurate than any other comparable historical text. Not only that, I became convinced that Jesus is who he says he is, the Son of God, fully God and fully man, and that he did the things the Bible claims he did. Initially, I didn't want to believe these things because they had profound implications for my life that I did not want to embrace. But I had to deal with the awkwardness of truth. I couldn't dismiss it just because it was uncomfortable. It resisted fitting neatly into the categories I wanted to fit it into. Truth is stubborn like that: it refuses to go away, no matter how much initially you may want to believe something else. It is verifiable.

I am not expecting you to hold the same perspective about Jesus Christ. What I *am* saying is that the claim that the truth about God, and therefore the truth about the world, is grounded in the person of Jesus Christ means that this claim can be assessed, evaluated, looked into and verified. It is not an exercise of mental effort to make yourself believe something in spite of reality; it is a sober-minded engagement *with* reality.

- First, we can look at the integrity of Jesus' life. Do the virtues that he espouses ring true in his life? Is his life attractive and authentic? Do the high ideals he teaches stack up with his actions?
- Second, if you find yourself saying, 'OK, his life may be attractive but is it true?', you can apply the normal standards of truth to Jesus because he is not just an abstract ideal or a private religious experience; he is a person who really lived, and there is a huge body of evidence to be engaged with.

The issue, as G. K. Chesterton commented, is too often that 'the Christian ideal has not been tried and found wanting. It has been found difficult; and left untried'.[8]

The challenge of truth

Finally, as we seek to know the truth, we must not be naive about how we respond to the truth ourselves. We often like to think that we are 'on the side of truth' and so when we encounter the truth about ourselves, the world or God then of course we will accept it. Dare I say, that is very naive.

Dan Ariely, in his book *The (Honest) Truth about Dishonesty*, highlights research that shows that most of us are willing to cheat, given the temptation or opportunity – we are just not willing to admit that we do. We cheat just a little, enough to pass unnoticed and (importantly) to convince ourselves that we aren't really being dishonest. This 'fudge factor' is the key. We want to cheat (to benefit from it) but we also want to think of ourselves as honest people. So we resolve the conflict by 'cognitive flexibility' (or self-deception, as it could be called!). 'We convince ourselves we are moral by the standards we hold, but we are happy to break those standards, so long as we convince ourselves that we haven't!'[9]

If you are resisting this analysis then imagine I were to ask you, 'Are you a liar?' I am sure you would say, 'No!' But then reflect on how many times you actually do lie. Of course, like me, you probably explain them away as 'white lies', insignificant, a bit of exaggeration, not as bad as others, etc. All well-documented psychological tactics for avoidance: justification, minimizing, distraction. And isn't that exactly the point? You've lied but have convinced yourself you haven't. On a more significant level I remember reading an interview with Amaryllis Fox, who worked for the CIA in counterterrorism and intelligence, often undercover. She said, 'If I learned one thing in my time working with the CIA, it is this, everyone believes they are the good guy.' Once again this highlights the way we like to think that we are on the side of truth, but that belief itself usually flies in the face of reality.

We often like to think that we are 'truth seekers': *Just show me the truth and I'll believe it.* Therefore, if I don't believe something, the problem must be lack of information. That can sometimes be the case, but often the problem is not lack of information but lack of inclination. What if the thing that someone is claiming is true has big implications for my life? What if I don't *want* it to be true? Thomas Cranmer was one of the founding theologians of the Church of England and he taught (as summarized by Cranmer expert Ashley Null) that what the heart loves, the will chooses and the intellect justifies. In other words, we are led more by our hearts than by our heads. If you have ever known an addict or tried to persuade a friend that the man/woman they are attracted to is going to be bad for them then you will know how true this statement is. We follow our desires and then deploy our intellect to justify the decision. Therefore, can I encourage you as you read on to be attentive to your heart? An honest engagement with truth requires some self-reflection. Is the problem really lack of information or is it lack of inclination on your part?

Grace and truth

Something that helps us to become more truthful is when we realize that Jesus is described in John 1:14 as being 'full of grace and truth'. Notice he is not half truth and half grace – a fifty/fifty split – but full of both, a glorious holistic integration. What that means is that, as God, he knows the truth about everything, and that includes you and me. He knows you, the real you. The high ideals and your fallen realities. The gap between your expectations and your actions. He knows your half-truths and the lies that are told to advance your agenda, to plump up your image or to deflect from your failings. He sees you at your best and he sees you at your worst. He sees you, the real you. He sees us behind the masks that we all put on, behind all the filters and the online profiles. He is full of truth.

But he is also full of grace, because what does he do with that truth about you? To have the full truth about anyone is to have enormous power over them. An old magazine from 1897 called *Tit-Bits* relates that Sir Arthur Conan Doyle (the creator of Sherlock Holmes) heard of an archdeacon who, it was claimed, was above reproach. Mischievously, Conan Doyle decided to put this to the test, dispatching a telegram to the revered gentlemen saying, 'All is discovered; fly at once!' The archdeacon promptly disappeared.[10]

Well, in a similar way, how does Jesus use the truth about you? Does he use it to expose you, to shame, manipulate and control you? No, because he is full of grace. He takes the painful truths about you, your lies, your deceptions, the things you don't want anyone to find out, and, although he is the only person who has ever lived a perfect life of truth, he died on a cross 2,000 years ago to pay for all those things for you. He, the source of all truth, died for our lies. He, who lived a perfect life of integrity, died for our deception.

Because of this the pastor and anti-Nazi dissident Dietrich Bonhoeffer once wrote:

> The cross is God's truth about us, and therefore it is the only power which can make us truthful. When we know the cross, we are not afraid of the truth.[11]

He is saying that if someone knew you, the real you, warts and all, and at that moment loved you unconditionally and forgave you everything, wouldn't that then make you uniquely honest and unafraid of the truth? For what would you fear? The truth? No, you would now be able to be truthful about yourself, probably for the first time.

Truth is very powerful. We all know that the pen is mightier than the sword because it is the stroke of the pen that causes armies to march and regimes to tumble. We have considered in this chapter that a big part of our erosion of truth and the creation of the facts/value dichotomy has been our fear that truth claims are power plays. But we have also seen that such a shift in the grounds of truth doesn't work. So what is the alternative? We need to reintegrate truth by seeing it grounded in personhood and supremely in the person of Jesus Christ. He shows us that truth is there to be used graciously (notice the integration of facts and values), to liberate and heal for the good of the other, not to enslave and harm for our own personal ends. In a context where the public discourse is too often characterized by lies, slander and a 'cancel culture', isn't this a much-needed corrective?

Can you see that if Jesus Christ is 'full of grace and truth', then knowing the truth about God should never make you arrogant? Often people fixate on any religious claim of exclusivity or uniqueness as the problem because we want to say that 'all opinions are equally valid'. But when Einstein discovered that energy and mass are interchangeable, expressed in his famous equation $E=mc^2$, he of course had discovered that by implication all those scientists with different theories at the time were wrong (and there were a number!). Did that necessarily make him suddenly arrogant and a bigot? Obviously not. Similarly, we have said, people are fearful of any claim to have 'the truth', particularly about God, and particularly if it might imply that others with different claims are wrong. But we have also seen that we can't escape truth claims. So how can we make a claim to religious truth without being arrogant, proud and dismissive, particularly of those who disagree with us?

Well, if the encounter with the truth about God has also been an encounter with grace, wouldn't that make all the difference? If God has graciously exposed the truth about you, your moral failures and your lies, and has forgiven you, then how could there be pride and arrogance? Surely such gracious truth would humble you and make you kinder and more compassionate to others. Surely the very truth you fervently believe about yourself and God is, in this case, inherently humbling? Think of it this way: as a Christian, knowing the 'truth' about yourself and God does not mean that you think you are morally or religiously better than anyone else. In fact it is the opposite. To be a Christian means that you have accepted God's diagnosis of the truth about the human condition and about yourself, which is that you are deeply morally flawed (what the Bible calls 'sinful'), and prone to lying and deceit. Is that not inherently humbling? Does that not mean that you would have strong reasons for thinking that others would most likely be more moral than you, and therefore should you not be quicker to listen to others and slower to commend yourself? How could that lead to arrogance?

At the same time, such an awareness of your sin wouldn't take away your concern for truth, would it? If anything, it would increase it. It would make you passionately eager to be an agent of truth in the world, and to lie and deceive no longer, because you see how much truth matters. If truth matters so much to God that he was prepared to send his Son, Jesus Christ, to die for it, then, as someone who lives in the light of that, surely you would become passionate about truth. You would become an advocate for truth, becoming much more honest about yourself. This truthful and gracious mode of engagement is something we intuitively find very attractive but very hard to achieve; it is something which is too often lacking in the emotionalism that characterizes our public debates. Wonderfully, it is something that is available to all by rediscovering the vital place of God in our understanding of truth – a God who is full of grace and truth.

Jesus paints for us the beautifully integrated and balanced picture of a just world, a new society, the kingdom of heaven in glorious technicolour.

3

Morality

How do we make the world a better place?

The good life

In the West today, two of our main concerns are morality and happiness. We long to make the world a better place and we long to be happy. Think of the kind of Instagram or Facebook post that people love to share (and which secretly might make you feel a bit nauseous):

> Just climbed Mt Kilimanjaro for charity; look at that sunrise #Happy #Blessed

It's pretty much the socially perfect post, isn't it? Moral but not preachy, happy but not selfish, improving the world and having a great time doing it! Surely this is the good life.

The author Fyodor Dostoevsky wrote, in his classic work *The Brothers Karamazov*:

> For the secret of man's being is not only to live but to have something to live for. Without a stable conception of the object of life, man would not consent to go on living, and would rather destroy himself than remain on earth, though he had bread in abundance.[1]

It is significant that this quote comes in a section of the book where Ivan is telling a story to his brother Alyosha to argue that the vast

49

majority of humanity cannot handle the freedom that God has given them and would live better were that freedom taken away. For centuries, humanity has grappled with this question of how we should use our freedom. Today we have unparalleled freedom in our society but are struggling to articulate how we should use it. The two dominant answers to this question are, arguably, morality and happiness. We should use our freedom to improve the world and we should use our freedom to be happy.

Historically, these two areas have been explored under one banner, 'The Good Life'. Many philosophers such as Plato and Kant have argued that morality and happiness are actually in competition, and so we have to choose one or the other. To do what is right we have to sacrifice our pursuit of happiness. That, they argued, is the good life. Others, most notably Aristotle, argued that if we think rightly about these two areas then they are not in competition but are actually compatible. We can live a moral life and we can live a happy life at the same time. For the West, this is the Holy Grail. That's why those social media posts make us jealous but also get so many 'likes': the happy and moral person! But, like the Holy Grail in the old stories, we are finding that this good life is elusive.

In this chapter we will think more about morality and the question of how we make the world a better place, and in the next we'll consider happiness. As we do so, we will consider whether the two might be compatible and whether we might be able to become the happy and moral people we long to be.

A longing for justice

There is lots of evidence that the current generation of young adults is particularly concerned about social justice. This is the generation of Black Lives Matter and #MeToo. Think of the importance of social and environmental issues such as global warming, poverty, displaced people groups and minority rights. These issues feature particularly prominently in young adults' voting patterns.

But it is not just politics; the longing for justice also affects their views on business and work. The World Economic Forum Global Shapers Survey surveyed 31,000 people worldwide under the age of thirty (the age group accounting for 50% of the world's population) and found that this cohort has a particularly strong conscience when it comes to social issues and expects companies to address social and environmental concerns: most (66.2%) disagree strongly or somewhat strongly with the statement, 'Companies should not be involved in addressing social problems that are not related to their business activities', and a higher percentage than ever before look for purpose and social impact in their work (40%).[2]

This may seem uncontroversial to you as you read it. 'Of course politics should be concerned with addressing social problems and businesses should care about corporate social responsibility (CSR).' But it has not always been so. Previous generations were much more concerned with political and social stability, the growth of the economy and raising a family. Of course, some in every generation have cared about justice, but its prominence today, the over-riding desire shared by so many to 'make the world a better place', is new.

Problems agreeing on justice

While pretty much everyone will say they are 'for justice' in general terms, anyone who has studied a bit of social or political theory will know that terms such as justice are highly contested. Justice is a word that implies a vision for a world functioning rightly, but what is that vision? Fifty yards away from my church in London is the Marx Memorial Library. It is the building that Lenin worked in from 1902–1903 to edit the communist publication *The Spark* (you can still go to the office that he used), and it was in this building that the first English editions of Marx's *Das Kapital* were printed. Still today, every 1 May, socialists crowd into Clerkenwell Green waving red flags with pictures of Lenin and Marx and march for socialism. Communism/socialism has a particular view of what a just world looks like. Is this the right view of justice? Or is it a liberal vision of justice, or a conservative vision? Is it the vision of political theorist John Locke or that of Jean-Jacques Rousseau? What is the just vision for the world that will make it a better place? You get the point: justice is a highly contested term.

Social psychologist Jonathan Haidt, in his book *The Righteous Mind*, argues that over time we have developed six moral tastes, a bit like the way the tongue tastes sweet, sour, salty, bitter, etc. He identifies these six tastes as: care/harm, fairness/inequality, loyalty/betrayal, authority/order, sanctity/purity and liberty/oppression.[3]

What is fascinating is how Haidt shows from his research that different social, religious and political groups make decisions about morality and justice by emphasizing certain moral tastes. Liberals see justice in terms of fairness/inequality and liberty/oppression but hardly give any weight to the moral categories of loyalty or sanctity. This means that when making decisions about whether a thing is right or wrong, if it can't be shown to have an impact on liberty or fairness, or it doesn't have much bearing on those considerations, liberals show very little concern for it. It is the same for any group; each one prefers certain moral tastes and, therefore, many of our disputes about justice are merely expressing our different emphases on different tastes.

But this of course raises a key question, and one which Haidt can't and doesn't answer: what does a balanced moral palate look like?

Is there right and wrong?

Some may say, 'Well, there *is* no absolute balanced moral palate because there is no absolute right and wrong. You have just shown it through Haidt's work; it is all just subjective. We are merely expressing our different cultural perspectives and preferences.'

There are a number of problems with this position. First, it certainly doesn't seem that at face value all moral judgments are subjective. Try as you might, it is really difficult to believe that egregious acts of evil, such as, say, the Holocaust or the Rwandan genocide, aren't actually morally wrong but are just an expression of social consensus. Historically, when we stand against such events and even when we appraise them today, we don't use the language of opinion or consensus; we use the language of objective morality. We call them 'wrong', 'evil' and 'unjust', and rightly so.

Second, when we make moral statements we certainly do not ordinarily think we are merely expressing preferences. Preferences and morality are very different categories, and even a young child can grasp the distinction between them. When my son says, 'I want you to give me ice cream', he knows he is saying something very different from when he says, 'You *should* give me ice cream' (because, for example, I made him a promise that I would). He may try to shift from preference to moral judgment to give his argument greater force (a good tactic that both children and adults employ!), but that just serves to reinforce the point that they are different statements with different weight behind them. Preference is individual. Morality is universal. Preference is an expression of personal desire. Morality is an expression of a binding moral law.

This is an important point to dwell on, because it is common today for people to assert that we can have moral principles, which historically have come from Christianity, but we can base them on non-Christian, secular humanist foundations. The argument is sometimes framed like this: what we call morality today is just a shared set of preferences that have been seen, over time, to be of evolutionary or social benefit to us as a whole. But they are not themselves referring to any binding moral laws.

We looked at this to a degree in the 'Origins' chapter, when we considered the many human rights we take for granted that flow from a view of humanity as the image of God. Can't we have one without the other?

W. H. Auden, the eminent twentieth-century poet, grew up in a Christian context but became a liberal humanist in his early adulthood. He too believed that he could keep his Christian morals but base them on liberal humanist principles. In November 1939 he went to a German-language cinema in New York. It was showing an official German newsreel celebrating the Nazi victory over Poland. (Up to the point when the United States and Germany declared war, German films could be shown in American theatres.) Auden was shocked by the shouts of 'Kill the Poles!' from an audience of ordinary German immigrants who were under no coercion to support the Nazis. Many years later he told an interviewer:

> I wondered, then, why I reacted as I did against this denial of every humanistic value. The answer brought me back to the church.[4]

In fact, the Nazis' rise to power in that same year, 1933, made large moral questions seem suddenly more urgent for him. He wrote later:

> The novelty and shock of the Nazis was that they made no pretense of believing in justice and liberty for all, and attacked Christianity on the grounds that to love one's neighbor as

54

oneself was a command fit only for effeminate weaklings . . . If, as I am convinced, the Nazis are wrong and we are right, what is it that validates our values and invalidates theirs?[5]

Auden made a very significant point. You can't just lift moral principles out of their framework and expect them to stand up. We may be passionate about a just world, but where have we got the idea of just and unjust, right and wrong from? As C. S. Lewis memorably argued:

A man does not call a line crooked unless he has some idea of a straight line. What was I comparing this universe with when I called it unjust? . . . If the whole universe has no meaning, we should never have found out that it has no meaning.[6]

So the question that is often asked by secular humanists, 'Why do we need God to tell us what is right and wrong?', is in part answered by these two aspects: first, is there actually any such thing as right and wrong and morality if there is no God? If it all just collapses into preference and opinion, even if expressed by many people or indeed a whole society, then it doesn't seem to be morality as we believe it to be – a set of universal binding laws.

Second, in the West we have inherited centuries of ethics, which have been built upon a Christian and biblical framework.[7] If we are convinced that these moral precepts are right, but we remove the Christian framework in which they have sat for two thousand years, how can we stand against those like the Nazis, who, drawing on the philosophy of Friedrich Nietzsche, concluded that humility and forgiveness were weak vices to be dismissed, that all people are not in fact equal, and that those with physical or mental impairments need to be killed off and bred out of the human race before they weaken the gene pool? How would we argue that everyone should be educated and enjoy basic freedoms when they would argue that it will advance society and humanity better if just some are educated and the 'lesser' people do the hard manual labour as functional slaves who enable those who are ethnically and genetically 'better' to flourish? We may not like such conclusions. We may not want to reach their conclusions. But can we really claim that they and the other brutal secular regimes of the twentieth century, including Mao's China, Stalin's Russia and Pol Pot's Cambodia, just hadn't worked out their ethics consistently with their secular humanist principles? Isn't it more likely that we are the anomalies, clinging to Western, historically 'Christian' morality while trying to claim secular beliefs?

Fortunately, there is a way to argue against such troubling conclusions, but it is not by jettisoning God. Instead, it is by putting God back in his rightful place as the source of our morality and the one who commissions us to assist in his work to bring about a just world.

Bringing about a just world

In the Old Testament there are two principal words for justice, which often go hand in hand. The first word is *mishpat*. It comes from the Hebrew word *shaphat*, meaning 'to judge'. It paints a picture of a just society where all injustices are dealt with. It is a big-picture word, a vision for a just society, shaped by what the Bible calls 'the perfect law that gives freedom' (James 1:25). In technical terms it would usually be called 'rectifying justice'. The second word is *tsadiq* and is often translated as 'righteousness'. This is more concerned with the individual and relational level. It speaks to each person's responsibilities and obligations and their relationships with other people, which enable a just society to come about.[8]

One thing that is important to note is that today we have an overwhelming focus on rectifying justice but are almost entirely silent on our responsibilities and obligations to bring about a just world. Or, to put it another way, we are very good at articulating the standards of justice but have very little idea of how to put those standards into effect in our society.

An area where we see this particularly acutely is in the debate between rights and responsibilities. In 1948, on the back of two consecutive world wars, the United Nations General Assembly came together to publish the Declaration of Human Rights. Today it is a foundational document and a binding part of international law. However, rights are incoherent unless they are accompanied by corresponding responsibilities. So, if you have a right to freedom of speech, it functions only if I embrace my responsibility to let you speak. Or think of the rights of displaced people and refugees. They have a right to life (Article 2) and the right to liberty and shelter (Article 5), but who has the responsibility for enabling those rights? We may be very articulate in espousing human rights, but in Europe particularly one of the most painful human stories of the past few years has been the refusal of states to take on the associated responsibilities, as refugees have been turned back at the border no sooner than they have been rescued from overcrowded boats fleeing wartorn countries.

The Sermon on the Mount is Jesus Christ's main block of ethical teaching. You can read it in Matthew 5 – 7:27. If you have never read it, may I urge you to do so? It is breathtaking in its scope, unrivalled in its beauty and remarkable in its depth but also in its simplicity. It is difficult to overstate its impact on Western society as our foundational ethical text. The uniting idea of Jesus' sermon is his repeated phrase, 'the kingdom of heaven'. It is a strange phrase to us, but it was a powerful and evocative vision to the original hearers. It speaks of a kingdom – a sphere of authority. Intuitively we all know that those who have authority over us are significant, whether a parent, or a sports coach, or a prime minister or president. The better the leader, the more wise and good they are, and the more powerful they are, then the greater and better their influence. Similarly, in speaking of the 'kingdom of heaven' or 'the kingdom of God', as Jesus sometimes phrases it, he is asking us to imagine what it would be like if God were to use all of his wisdom, goodness and holy power to effect change in the world and in our lives. Wouldn't that be utterly transformative?

But Jesus doesn't leave us just to guess what that would look like. The Sermon on the Mount paints in vivid brush strokes the big-picture vision of this new society. It is a place where those who mourn are comforted, where those who are poor in spirit are blessed, where the hungry are fed and the downtrodden are lifted up. It speaks to the spiritual life of this new society: its social dynamics include restoration and forgiveness, generosity and debt relief, the importance of the home and responding to violence and injustice, to mention but a few areas.

Wonderfully, however, the Sermon on the Mount also articulates our individual responsibilities and the relational dynamics (the *tsadiq*) that enable such big-picture (*mishpat*) justice. With remarkable economy of words Jesus teaches about the virtues we need to cultivate to become the type of people through whom God will work to foster the 'kingdom of heaven': poverty of spirit, meekness, mercy, purity of heart, peacemaking (Matthew 5:3–10). He talks about how these virtues can be cultivated by our internal spiritual life (Matthew 6:1–21). And he shows us the actions that need to be worked out in our relationships: persistence in pursuing what is right (even when it leads to persecution), self-control, reconciliation, forgiveness, faithfulness and radical generosity (Matthew 5:11–48).

One fascinating test to do with Jesus' teaching here is to compare it with Haidt's moral tastes: care/harm, fairness/inequality, loyalty/

betrayal, authority/order, sanctity/purity and liberty/oppression. How does Jesus' picture of the kingdom of heaven compare?

- *Care/harm* – yes, he urges a profound concern for the vulnerable and the downtrodden.
- *Fairness/inequality* – yes, he is scrupulously detailed about standards of fairness and profoundly challenging about equality across gender, ethnic and socio-economic lines.
- *Loyalty/betrayal* – yes, he advocates the highest standards of commitment to one another and our vows.
- *Authority/order* – yes, there is a clear articulation of a social order and validation of authorities as being essential to society's proper functioning.
- *Sanctity/purity* – yes, purity of heart is one of the key virtues that is worked out in many different social relationships, such as marriage and the family.
- *Liberty/oppression* – yes, the hungry are fed, the captives are liberated and the oppressed are raised up and restored.

In other words, if you evaluate Jesus and his teaching against Haidt's moral tastes, then Jesus shows us what a perfectly balanced moral palate looks like. How do we make the world a better place? Jesus paints for us the beautifully integrated and balanced picture of a just world, a new society, the kingdom of heaven in glorious technicolour.

Our need for something more than justice

I wonder how you felt as you read the brief exposition of Jesus' Sermon on the Mount above. If you are anything like me, you might have found yourself drawn to it, attracted by the picture that was being painted. At the same time, isn't there a part of you that withdraws because it is deeply challenging? Isn't there a part of you that wants to say, 'Sure, it sounds good, but isn't it a bit unrealistic?

Who could ever live this way?' I think it's a bit like if I were down at the park and having a knock around on the local tennis courts. I'm an OK amateur player, so let's imagine I'm having a good day and beating those I'm playing against. I might start to think, 'I'm a pretty good player.' Then imagine that Roger Federer turns up and says, 'Let's play a match.' On the one hand, it would be a great privilege and a thrill to play with him. On the other hand, I'd get thrashed and my ego would take a real beating. Suddenly I would see what 'good' really looks like and, much as I might admire it, I would also find it profoundly uncomfortable.

In Shakespeare's play *The Merchant of Venice*, in its seminal court scene, the character Portia warns Shylock, 'Though justice be thy plea, consider this: That in the course of justice none of us should see salvation.'[9] The point is a profound one. We might all long for justice and cry out for it, but we should pause and reflect on that desire. Justice must, by definition, be universal. This means that the standards of justice are not met if they are applied to some and not to others. That is bias and partiality: the opposite of justice. So, when we long to have a just and better world, we have to ask ourselves the uncomfortable question: how do we fare when *our* lives are put under the microscope of justice?

Intuitively, most of us respond by saying things like, 'I'm a good person; I'm not perfect but I'm not bad.' But is that actually true? In his recent book *The Character Gap*, Christian B. Miller goes through chapter after chapter of psychology studies to assess people's character. It is fascinating and uncomfortable reading. Miller shows that all the evidence is that while most of us are not monsters, neither can we claim to be the good and virtuous people we think we are. He looks in one chapter at 'Helping' and notes a study conducted by Cornell University. He describes how an actor was in a shop and had a shopping bag that had a rip in it, causing items to fall out of the bag. Of twenty adults who saw this, only three did anything to help. Seventeen (or 85%) did nothing, even though it would have been easy to do so. Are you surprised? Perhaps you think that's pretty trivial, a one-off? Miller writes about many similar studies all yielding the same results: most of us, even when it costs little to help, simply don't! And it's not only helping; Miller looks at lying, cheating, even harming, and finds time and again that there is a significant disjunction between how good we think we are and how good we *actually* are when it comes to 'The Character Gap'.[10]

This gap between the real and the ideal is what the Bible calls sin, and it is the main problem that hinders the just world we long to have. A number of different pictures are used in Scripture to describe this problem: an arrow missing a mark, a line being transgressed, an internal distortion away from our true purpose. But whether breaking a standard, falling short of a goal or failing to be the people we long to be, the analysis is the same. There's a character gap.

Often when we are asked to diagnose what is wrong with the world we point to factors 'out there'. Governments and big businesses failing to meet their carbon-neutral targets, capitalist systems perpetuating injustice by failing to distribute wealth properly, the modern slavery scandal, for example. But then how many of us are complicit in these problems? Would our recycling and energy use stand up to careful scrutiny and show a deep and proper care for the environment? Would our consumption habits and charitable giving show a selfless approach or a selfish one to others? Would our browser history expose a use of pornography, which finances and perpetuates much of modern slavery? If justice is our plea, would any of us find salvation? Would a careful and just inventory of our lives not in fact leave us all facing judgment? We need something more.

Righteousness and peace kiss

There is a beautiful verse in Psalm 85 that memorably says that when God saves people, 'love and faithfulness meet together; righteousness and peace kiss each other' (Psalm 85:10). It is beautiful because, in this verse, apparently opposite qualities come together. 'Faithfulness' in the verse means a commitment to the truth, but if God knows the full truth about us and our character gap then would it be right for him still to love us? We have seen that 'righteousness' means being committed to doing what is right individually and in our relationships, but, given how far short we fall of that standard, should we expect peace between us and God?

This psalm and many other verses in the Old Testament set up a tension. God is just and he will not be partial and sweep wrongdoing under the carpet. But he is also merciful and compassionate, a God who loves us and wants *shalom* for us, a deep and rich peace. How can God hold these two in tension? Aren't they mutually exclusive?

The tension is wonderfully resolved at the cross of Jesus Christ. This is the moment in space, time and history when 'love and faithfulness meet together; righteousness and peace kiss each other'. God does not resolve the tension by playing one side off against the other. His commitment to love does not cancel out his faithfulness, nor does his desire for peace negate righteousness. Instead, in Jesus Christ, God the perfectly faithful one pays for our unfaithfulness. On the cross, in Jesus Christ, God the perfectly righteous one pays for our unrighteousness. He does this to love us and bring about peace between him and us.

In *The Merchant of Venice*, Portia goes on in her speech to Shylock to speak of mercy. It is one of the most beautiful sections of writing in all of Shakespeare's rich pantheon of plays:

The quality of mercy is not strained;
It droppeth as the gentle rain from heaven
Upon the place beneath: it is twice blest;
It blesseth him that gives and him that takes:
'Tis mightiest in the mightiest: it becomes
The throned monarch better than his crown;
His sceptre shows the force of temporal power,
The attribute to awe and majesty,
Wherein doth sit the dread and fear of kings;
But mercy is above this sceptred sway;
It is enthronèd in the hearts of kings,
It is an attribute to God himself;
And earthly power doth then show likest God's
When mercy seasons justice.[11]

Mercy is indeed an attribute of God himself. He gives us more than justice, much more. He gives us the blessing of mercy. He gives us his very own Son. Mercy is the glory of the crown upon God's head and the sceptre by which he rules; it is his very beating heart. We the unjust are forgiven because of his mercy.

How does this make a difference to our engagement in the world and how does it help to make the world a better place?

If the basic problem is not 'out there' but 'in here', in people like you and me who perpetuate injustice, then this really does get to the 'heart' of the problem. If we accept God's offer of mercy and forgiveness it works in our hearts, in the power of God's Spirit, to change us, for mercy properly received always leads to change.

Let me give you a trivial example. I am quite a stickler for time-keeping, so I don't like it when people are late for a meeting with me. If I'm honest, I have in the past been quite cold and dismissive to those who have been late, and I'm not proud of it. A few years ago a friend of mine was visiting from Japan. He's a busy guy, we had only an hour and a half to catch up and we hadn't seen each other for more than a year. We had arranged to meet at 10 am near Bank in London, and because he was keen to make the most of the time, he even texted me the night before to check we were still on for the meeting. I confirmed (but did think to myself, 'As if I'd miss this meeting!'). I got up in the morning and then completely forgot. When 10 am came, I was on the other side of London! I got a text at 10.15 am saying, 'Hi Pete, hope everything is alright; are you still coming?' I was mortified. I rushed across as quickly as I could but it took me forty-five minutes. I was an hour late and we had just thirty minutes together. But here's the amazing thing: as I walked into the café I was greeted by a gentle smile from my friend, and as I blurted out my apology he simply said, 'Pete, I totally forgive you; these things happen – we still have half an hour together.' He could have had a go at me; he could have said, 'But I confirmed with you last night!', but he didn't. Instantly his mercy restored me. So how do you think I react now when someone is late for me? Well, sadly I can still be frustrated, but I am way more understanding and merciful than I ever was before. However, this has not made me any less concerned about being on time. If anything, I care even more about it, because at that moment when I was late for my friend I felt its importance. But I am now (and I am trying to be!) kinder and more merciful to others.

This is a picture of how God's mercy works to change us. As we remember what he has done for us in and through Jesus Christ, it cultivates in us a kinder and more loving, merciful and compassionate disposition towards others. As Shakespeare wrote, 'Mercy seasons justice'. Crucially, it does this without diminishing our standards of justice. It actually *raises* them. We become more, not less, committed to *mishpat*, but as recipients of God's mercy we do so with a deeper commitment to becoming the type of righteous, *tsadiq* people to bring it about. That's the dynamic of mercy in the gospel of Jesus Christ that makes the world a better place.

There is a great difference between being alive and having something to live for.

4

Happiness

How can we be happy?

The pursuit of happiness

It is an old axiom that 'everyone should work out, before they die, what they are running from, and to, and why'. Whether consciously or not, in the West we spend an enormous amount of time running after happiness. During my research for this book, the question 'Where can I find true happiness?' was the most important one asked by friends of Christians (46.6% of those asked said their friends wanted to know the answer to this question). The well-known statement from the United States Declaration of Independence of 1776 that 'the pursuit of happiness' is, along with life and liberty, an 'unalienable right' has become a mantra for the West. In fact, it is so commonly accepted that if you were to ask someone, 'Are you pursuing happiness?' they might very well respond, 'What else is there to pursue?'

Think of the rise of the cupcake. Over the past decade it has become symbolic of our pursuit of happiness. A small foundation of nondescript sponge cake, overwhelmed by a mini mountain of thickly layered, brightly coloured buttercream on top. Cupcake shops have popped up everywhere: the street corner, the railway station, next to the bus stop. If you feel guilty about having a whole one, there are even mini-cupcakes to allay your fears. 'Go on, have one; it'll brighten up your day!' Is staff morale low at work? Buy them cupcakes! The erstwhile bastion of birthdays and special occasions has now become as commonplace as snacking on an apple, except that few do that any more. It's all part of our pursuit of happiness.

More of our income is spent on leisure than in previous generations, with the leisure sector in the UK on track to amount to £144bn in 2022, about 10% of disposable income, and it is higher at 11% in the US.[1] We have personalized browser experiences so that online interactions are tailored 'just for you'. Go into a Starbucks™ and ask for your drink of choice and you don't just get any drink; you get your own unique drink, with your name on it.

The pursuit of happiness is not necessarily a recent phenomenon but is something that can be traced back a couple of hundred years to the Romantic Movement around the turn of the nineteenth century. With an increasing focus on emotion and experience, there was a shift to a corresponding focus on happiness as the supreme good. For example, in ethics Percy Shelley argued that happiness was what defined morality: 'That is called good which produces pleasure, that is called evil which produces pain.'[2] Correspondingly, Jeremy Bentham argued that the pursuit of happiness should shape politics: 'Nature has placed mankind under the governance of two sovereign masters, pain and pleasure. It is for them alone to point out what we ought to do, as well as to determine what we shall do.'[3] Similarly, a little later, in the twentieth century, Freud claimed that happiness was the key to mental health through his 'pleasure principle': 'the driving force of the idea is the instinctual seeking of pleasure and the avoidance of pain.'[4] So happiness became the essential focus of morality, politics and psychology.

In many ways, this was not what the founding fathers who wrote the Declaration of Independence had envisaged. They were not trying to reshape society to make happiness the supreme good. Their focus was on making the freedom to pursue life, liberty and happiness available to *all*. They wanted a just and equitable society more than a happy society. Nonetheless, this pursuit of happiness is so ubiquitous in the West now that it is almost inconceivable that we would live for anything else. But, contrary to our prevailing view, many cultures throughout history and around the world today have pursued other goals: liberty, love, family, justice. So is happiness the right thing to pursue?

The paradox of the pursuit of happiness

Since so much energy and resources have been put into seeking happiness, it is important to ask whether this has worked. Well, on the one hand, if you look at reports measuring things such as the 'life satisfaction scores' of nations, then – broadly speaking – improvements in healthcare, living standards and economic prosperity *have* brought about better scores. Countries that are more developed and show better levels of health and education and higher incomes generally report higher life satisfaction. Therefore, as countries improve in these areas over time, it is not surprising to see life satisfaction scores also improving.[5]

But this is not the whole picture. Negative emotions are rising around the world and some of the countries where they are rising most sharply are those where life satisfaction scores are high. The World Happiness Report looks at a number of indicators, and one of its three key measures is 'negative affect', which looks at the average frequency of worry, sadness and anger on the previous day. Since 2005 the 'negative affect' across the world has been markedly and steadily rising, from 22% then to 28% in 2019.[6] In other words, the frequency of worry, sadness and anger among people in society has been increasing. This corresponds with numerous studies showing that mental ill health is on the rise. All this leads us to an important question: if, generally speaking, living standards are improving and therefore there is increasing life satisfaction, why is there a corresponding increase in unhappiness, anger, anxiety and mental ill health?

A number of commentators have suggested that these two trends (increasing life satisfaction and increased negative affect) are not just incidental but are essentially linked. Pointing to the increasing mental ill health epidemic in the US, where the rising use of anti-depressants makes them the most-used class of drugs among 18–44-year-olds, Bruce Levine argues that the pursuit of happiness and pleasure has had a dehumanizing effect on society. Therefore, the rise in mental ill health is a form of psychological rebellion against a culture that is so focused on happiness that it has become trivial and banal.[7] It is the mental equivalent of drinking cola and eating crisps and chocolate all day. It may taste good at the time, but ultimately it leaves you feeling sick and unhealthy. G. K. Chesterton, writing on the same theme, put it this way:

> Despair does not lie in being weary of suffering, but in being weary of joy. It is when for some reason or other the good things in a society no longer work that the society begins to decline; when its food does not feed, when its cures do not cure, when its blessings refuse to bless.[8]

Added to this there is the pressure to be happy. Pascal Bruckner writes in his book *Perpetual Euphoria*[9] that since there is so much focus on happiness and so many resources invested in it, then to fail to be happy is to fail completely. Think of something so obvious but so profound as the way we greet one another. In Britain the usual greeting used to be 'Good day', short for, 'I wish you a good day.' Now it has become, 'How are you?' It is as though the key thing we have to know about one another is our level of happiness. Of course, we all know the expected response, the words that, if you deviate too far from them, can really cause some social awkwardness: 'I'm fine.' Phew. I'm relieved to hear it!

Could it be that, although happiness is certainly important, we have elevated it too high? By making it the supreme pursuit, have we lost an important focus on other things? Might happiness be achieved not by pursuing it but by focusing on other, more worthy, goals?

What I want to suggest to you is that happiness is a 'shy virtue'; something which, if you go full-steam after it, will always elude you. But it is something that, if you patiently go about your life, living well and pursuing other more worthy ends, you will find has been by your side for some time. Our mistake has been that, by elevating a good thing like happiness into becoming the ultimate thing, we have lost sight of both morality and meaning. Paradoxically, Jesus Christ shows us that real happiness comes not by pursuing it directly, but by rediscovering how to live well and what we are living for.

Happiness and morality

Alongside our pursuit of happiness there has been a corresponding idea that the way to achieve happiness is to remove all constraints that might stop us getting it. Think of the way that liberals are often called progressives. This suggests that the way to progress is to liberate us from constraints. Put simply, an individual will be more likely to achieve happiness if they are freed from coercion and constraints and are allowed to shape their life as they choose. Bit by bit there has been a dismantling of restrictions in the steady march of progress towards the goal of happiness. The choice of the individual has become sovereign because of the underpinning belief that freedom to choose brings happiness.

In philosophy, however, this is only one half of what is usually thought of as 'freedom'. This view of freedom is 'freedom from' (technically called negative liberty), but the other side of freedom is 'freedom to' (positive liberty).[10] We understand the importance of this distinction in everyday life. If I want to run a marathon, I need to constrain my negative freedom about what I eat in order to achieve my positive freedom of being fit enough to run. Or consider marriage: if I want to be 'free' to have a happy marriage then I will need to limit my freedom by not having romantic relationships with other women. Indeed, I am very happy to constrain my freedom in that way, because the goal of loving my wife and having a happy and long-lasting marriage is so important to me.

The point is that the basic premise, that happiness is achieved by removing all constraints and allowing the individual to choose, is a glorious half-truth. Some constraints are important and necessary in order to help us achieve worthy ends – that's positive liberty.

This, therefore, has become a major problem in the West's pursuit of happiness. One by one, barriers have been pulled down, with little thought about what those barriers were there for. Of course, you would expect that if barriers are being torn down in a haphazard fashion then, just by the law of averages, in some situations that will be a good thing: barriers to women having equal opportunities at work, barriers to racial equality, for example. But, unsurprisingly, the removal of other barriers has had devastating consequences. Sexual liberalization at the expense of sexual fidelity within the context of marriage has led to a huge rise in divorces (from 5.9 per 1,000 marriages in 1971 to 14 per 1,000 in 2004),[11] and to about half of children being born outside marriage. This results in painful things like the fatherless generation (in 2011, 62% of all families in Camden, London – just a couple of miles north of where I live – had no dad present).[12] On the estate where I live in central London, single mothers do an amazing job under huge pressure, with too many fathers just not interested in being there for their kids and the family because they don't want to be 'tied down' or 'constrained' (notice the language).

In the same way, moral constraints have generally been seen as restrictions on desires and therefore restrictions on happiness. This has led to criticism of Christianity for being 'overly restrictive' and depriving us of happiness. Set against the culture's mantra, 'If it feels good, do it' (occasionally with the rider 'as long as it doesn't hurt anyone else'), any appeal to a moral law does look restrictive. But again this falls into the same error about freedom *from* and freedom *to*. Think of it like this: if I climbed up a couple of floors of a building and got ready to jump out of a window, I would hope that one of my friends would try to stop me. 'Pete, what about the law of gravity? If you jump you will fall and break all your bones.'

Imagine if I replied, 'Don't constrain me. I don't believe in the law of gravity. I just want to be free to fly.' If I jumped, we all know what would happen. Like it or not, I would be constrained by the law of gravity and would crash down to earth, breaking myself on it.

Just as there are physical laws, so God has put in place moral laws. And not because he is a killjoy or wants to 'suppress' our desires. In the Bible, God's moral law is called 'the perfect law that gives freedom' (James 1:25). That is, God has put in place certain constraints because he understands they are important to help us to be *free to* live in a way that makes for human flourishing. A society with no laws is not free but is anarchy; in the same way, living without reference to God and his moral laws causes a form of anarchy in our lives and means that we end up breaking ourselves on the boundaries he has put in place for our protection and our flourishing.

Similarly, our pursuit of happiness, with little or no thought given to the moral framework that God has ingrained in our world for our good, is actually making us less free. It is like Oscar Wilde's story of Dorian Gray,[13] who, having purchased eternal youth at the cost of his soul, pursued pleasure with no thought to its impact on others, while with every selfish choice the painting on his wall at home, showing his true self, bore more and more of the signs of his corruption. Part of the malaise we have in the West – the negative emotions we feel despite all our improvements in living standards – is a warning to us that we live without reference to God's moral law at our peril. Our souls will bear the scars.

We need to rediscover what our liberty is for and understand the appropriate constraints on freedom that God has put in place for our good.

Happiness and purpose

There is a great difference between being alive and having something to live for. We have already been thinking about the impact on the West of having lost sight of this. In his book *Amusing Ourselves to Death*, Neil Postman explores the difference between two seminal works, George Orwell's *1984* and Aldous Huxley's *Brave New World*. He writes:

Orwell feared we would become a captive culture. Huxley feared we would become a trivial culture ... As Huxley re-marked in Brave New World Revisited, the civil libertarians and rationalists who are ever on the alert to oppose tyranny 'failed to take into account man's almost infinite appetite for distraction.' In 1984, Orwell's people are controlled by in-flicting pain. In Brave New World, they are controlled by inflicting pleasure. In short, Orwell feared that what we hate will ruin us. Huxley feared that what we love will ruin us. This [book] is about the possibility that Huxley, and not Orwell, was right.[14]

Therefore, if we are to avoid the triviality of merely 'amusing ourselves to death', what *are* we to live for?

In a famous incident in chapter 4 of John's Gospel, Jesus meets a woman at a well and ends up speaking to her about the meaning of life. She may have lived 2,000 years ago but she faced many of the problems we have been grappling with in this chapter. She has been pursuing personal fulfilment, with little or no regard to the moral framework God put in place, by having a series of marriages and divorces (five in total). When Jesus meets her she is living with a man to whom she is not married. No doubt she thought that each relationship would make her happy. But, as Jesus says to her, drawing on the metaphor of water and the well, this has just left her thirsting for something to satisfy her fully.

She is taken aback that Jesus, as a Jewish man, would talk to her because she is a Samaritan woman and, in the ancient Middle East, men didn't speak to women in public and Jews hated Samaritans because of historical ethnic tensions. But Jesus is happy to overturn barriers such as sexism and racism that are wrongly limiting social freedom. When the conversation gets on to personal territory concerning her relationships, she tries to evade it by bringing up a controversy that was hot at that time between Jews and Samaritans about the correct location for worship. 'Our ancestors worshipped on this mountain, but you Jews claim that the place where we must worship is in Jerusalem' (John 4:20). Jesus could have said to her, 'Don't change the subject; we were just getting somewhere.' But instead he allows the apparent change of direction to continue, because he perceives something that she doesn't, namely that worship is actually the key point.

Worship may seem like a limited religious activity for a pious few, but Scripture's view of it is much more expansive. Worship (literally, 'worth-ship') is the act of assigning ultimate value or worth to something. It is about the fundamental orientation of our desires, the thing or things we think are most important and which we look to for meaning. Deep down, everyone has at least one thing that they believe will give them ultimate meaning and value. Whether you would use this language or not, this is what you worship. The woman has seemingly been looking to men and relationships to give her purpose and meaning, but each successive relationship has failed to satisfy her. Some think that popularity or approval, perhaps by getting enough followers or 'likes' on social media, will give them meaning, but then they find that followers are fickle and no matter how many they have, it is never enough and someone else always has more. Others look to the pursuit of a career for ultimate significance. In my time as a pastor I have sat with numerous people, working in the City, sometime after they have 'made it' by becoming a partner in the firm or getting the promotion they had told themselves would be 'enough'. The realization, at that point, that it is just another false horizon, that it was good but doesn't satisfy, can be crushing.

Jesus makes several important comments to the woman about worship:

> 'A time is coming and has now come when the true worship-pers will worship the Father in the Spirit and in truth, for they are the kind of worshippers the Father seeks. God is spirit, and his worshippers must worship in the Spirit and in truth.'
> The woman said, 'I know that Messiah' (called Christ) 'is coming. When he comes, he will explain everything to us.'
> Then Jesus declared, 'I, the one speaking to you – I am he.'
> (John 4:23–26)

He is telling her that her problem is she has been worshipping the wrong thing. She has been neglecting her true purpose. And what is that? To worship the Father in Spirit and in truth. This means that true purpose is found in placing ultimate value in knowing God as our Father, as he has truly revealed himself to be, and in enjoying that relationship with him. What is the meaning of life? To find ultimate value in and enjoy our relationship with God, our Father in heaven, who made us and loves us.

This realization changes everything for the woman. She is overjoyed.

> Then, leaving her water jar, the woman went back to the town and said to the people, 'Come, see a man who told me every-thing I've ever done. Could this be the Messiah?'
> (vv. 28–29)

Notice the small but significant detail, 'leaving her water jar'. Every day, that woman would have had to trudge to the well to fill up her bucket so that she could have water to drink to get her through another day. But the water always ran out. Jesus used the metaphor of water to highlight her existential thirst. How many times had she gone to a man to try to quench her thirst for meaning and purpose? But that water always ran out. It was never enough. Now, having found her true purpose, she leaves the water jar behind, because she doesn't need it any more. Her thirst has been quenched.

So it is for us: because God is infinite, being made to find our true purpose in him means that nothing else can satisfy us. That is why the great African theologian Augustine famously said, 'You have made us for yourself, O Lord, and our hearts are restless until they find their rest in you.'[15] Good things treated as the ultimate in our lives will always disappoint us and leave us restless. But, if we look to God to give us ultimate purpose, then our thirst for meaning and significance is quenched. And that means that we can now enjoy the good things of life, such as friends, family, a job, material possessions, a desire for significance, but we don't need to try to squeeze ultimate purpose out of them. That is something they could never provide and which always leads to our thirsting for more.

It also means that we now have purpose, and what a purpose it is! If life is not just about being alive but about knowing what to live for, then what could be greater or more significant than knowing God? And not just knowing him in an abstract way but knowing him truly and intimately as a Father who loves us? I know that all of us have had mixed experiences of our fathers, and sadly for some the concept of a father may even have negative associations, but the pain of that merely highlights what we all know intuitively: that a good father who loves us and is always there for us is an essential foundation for life. To worship God in truth is to come to know him as that loving Father who will never leave us or forsake us.

You may well ask, 'How can you be sure? How can you be sure that worshipping God satisfies and can give the meaning and purpose we are searching for? How can you be sure that God is actually there, as a good Father who will never leave us or forsake us?'

The whole interaction between Jesus and the woman at the well starts with him asking her, 'Will you give me a drink?' As the conversation plays out, however, she never actually gives him that drink. Instead, at a truer and deeper level, he quenches *her* thirst by providing her with the ultimate meaning she craves. In the end she goes away satisfied, but Jesus is still thirsty. That is just a small but significant picture of the gospel. John's account of Jesus' death is the only one where it is recorded that on the cross Jesus says, 'I am thirsty' (John 19:28). It is one of Jesus' famous seven 'last words'. Jesus is left thirsty so that we might have our ultimate thirst satisfied by a relationship with God. On the cross, Jesus doesn't just face physical thirst (though the agonizing dehydration as he bleeds to death would be bad enough), but he faces cosmic thirst. He, the divine Son, is cut off from his Father for our sake because of all the ways that we have worshipped idols – created things given to us by God but not intended to be ultimate in our lives. He faces God's just judgment for the ways that we have pursued happiness with no thought given to God's moral law; hurting others, hurting God's world, hurting ourselves and hurting God himself in the process. Jesus is rejected by his Father for all the ways we have rejected God and pushed him out of our lives to search for meaning in other things. And as Jesus does this, for us, he offers us the true and living water of his love that alone can satisfy.

As the words of the hymn go:

> On the mount of crucifixion,
> Fountains opened deep and wide;
> From the floodgates of God's mercy,
> Flowed a vast and gracious tide.
> Grace and love, like mighty rivers,
> Poured incessant from above,
> And heav'n's peace and perfect justice
> Kissed a guilty world in love.[16]

Beyond happiness to joy

Scripture places more emphasis on joy than on happiness. Happiness is something that is relatively superficial and transient, whereas joy is deeper and more permanent.

- Joy is greater than mere circumstances can provide (Psalm 4:7).
- It is also not dependent on circumstances (Philippians 4:4–7) and therefore can't be taken away from us.
- It can be experienced in the midst of trials and suffering (James 1:2; 1 Peter 1:6) even when we are faced with our own death (Philippians 2:17–18).

This is not some glib, happy-clappy faith that merely masks deep hurt. Nor is it a kind of Stoicism, gritting our teeth and pressing on. This is an emotionally engaged realism, which faces the pain of the world but ultimately finds its emotional centre in God. And since the relationship with God is permanent, enduring whatever the circumstances, even enduring through death, there is joy available no matter what we face. Isn't this what we all want?

The key to realizing this joy is, as I suggested earlier in the chapter, not to pursue it directly. Instead, we pursue the meaningful life – knowing God and worshipping him in all we do, and we also pursue the moral life by living according to God's ways, seeking to make the world a better place. As meaning and morality come together then we get a profound sense of joy.

This resolves the tension with which we started the previous chapter. We commented on the way that often the 'good life' (making the world a better place) and the 'happy life' are seen as standing in tension with each other because we think that to do good we have to sacrifice our happiness for the sake of another person and 'do the right thing'. So how can we be moral without being miserable, or happy without being selfish? If joy is to be found not through just pursuing my happiness but by pursuing ultimate meaning in a relationship with God and living his way, then this tension is reconciled.

Think of it as like playing in an orchestra. If ultimately I am convinced that I have to do what is good for *me* to be happy, then I will be like someone in an orchestra playing with no reference to others. This will just produce disharmony, frustration and sadness as I play my part but am at odds with others. But if there is a conductor (God) who sets the overall agenda for the orchestra and orders how we play together, drawing out our individual gifts and encouraging us to listen to one another as we help one another flourish, then suddenly our joy is not competitive. In fact, our joy is mutually reinforcing. I delight in your good by seeing you realize your gifts, as you do with me. We all then delight in the overall goal of why we are playing as the piece comes together in joyful harmony.

My joy is therefore accentuated by not turning in on myself but looking up to God and out to others. This is why Jesus said that the two greatest commandments are to 'love the Lord your God with all your heart and with all your soul and with all your mind' and to 'love your neighbour as yourself' (Matthew 22:37–39). Meaning and morality combine to produce a life of joy. Ultimately, that *is* the good life.

Christianity is not a call to find your identity by a religion or system of belief but an invitation to receive an identity from God.

5

Identity

What is the essence of who we are?

The question of identity

'You never get a second chance to make a first impression.' A few years ago, the shampoo brand Head and Shoulders ran an ad campaign with this strapline. It was brilliant in the way it played on a deep-seated fear we all have about our identity. It is the first-day-of-school syndrome: 'What if I make a mistake when meeting someone for the first time? What will they think of me? Will I forever be known as *that* person?' You never get a second chance to make a first impression.

Talking about identity is challenging because, although it is the essence of who we are, it is very difficult to examine. Think of it as a bit like looking at a photo of yourself and someone asking you to describe the camera that took the photo. Of course, the camera is essential to the photo; it is the lens through which the photo was shot. Most likely you were looking right at it when the photo was taken, but did you really notice it? How often do we stop to think about the camera? How often do we stop to think about our identity?

And yet I would go as far as to say that it is one of the most important questions facing the West today. Think of the prominence of 'identity politics'. Think of the huge and important debates around sex and gender, race, and sexual preference that have dominated the political landscape over the past decade. Think of the opportunities, particularly online, to construct your identity through your profile. Think of the advertising slogans urging you to 'Just be you' or 'You do you' or 'Be true to yourself' or 'Redefine yourself'. Identity is a fiercely relevant question for us today.

The Danish philosopher Søren Kierkegaard thought about identity a lot. He perceptively commented that if we form our identity in the wrong way, or base it on the wrong thing, then it is not just 'a mistake' but it is in some sense '*the* mistake', because it affects everything. But, he also reflected, it is a mistake that can go unnoticed, despite its huge implications. He wrote:

> The biggest danger of all, that of losing one's self, can occur very quietly in the world, as if it were nothing at all. No other loss can occur so quietly; any other loss – an arm, a leg, five dollars, a wife – is sure to be noticed.[1]

What is unique about our cultural moment is the possibility, never known before, to construct identity. Think of the challenge you face when setting up a social media profile. How do you present yourself? Authentic but not a mess, confident but not arrogant, beautiful/ handsome but not superficial, moral but not self-righteous, popular but not at the whim of the crowd . . . It is so difficult.

A while back there was a #NoFilter campaign, pushing back on the photoshopping of images and the pressure it puts, particularly on young people, to have the perfect body and face. My wife and I shared a laugh at what our photos would have looked like in comparison with the images of some of the celebrities posting photos using this hashtag, because they still looked stunning, and, while no doubt they are beautiful people, huge work had clearly been put into the right shot, in the right light, from the right angle, getting their best side – all for a campaign about showing people the 'real you'. That's the dilemma of identity formation right there.

Identity narratives

As we seek to construct our identity, there are, broadly speaking, two dominant narratives that underpin this 'identity project'. One is 'Just be yourself' or 'Be true to yourself'. Let's call that the 'modern' identity narrative (as in the narrative attached most obviously to the culture of modernity). The other is 'Be whoever you want to be' or 'Make something of yourself'. Let's call that the 'post-modern' identity narrative.

These two narratives are hugely important and influential. The first narrative, 'Just be yourself', draws on strong themes of liberty and emancipation. Within it lies the idea of external constraints holding someone back from being who they truly are. For many who are black or from an ethnic minority, this has been a key part of their struggle; it is the struggle of freedom from oppression, borne out in the longing to cry, 'Free at last, free at last.' But it is not only part of their story; it is also true that for many women this is a key theme in their struggle for women's rights. You hear it clearly in their experiences of being forced to conform to norms and structures of the majority culture that don't allow them to be who they really are and to enjoy the rights that should be theirs. Whether it is women having to put up with sexism at work because to speak up or do something about it would be to hinder their career, or a black person seeking to break free from prejudice and structural injustices, the point is that, for them, society is not a place where they can be 'true' to themselves.

This emancipation theme also features strongly in coming-out stories from members of the gay community. Freddie Mercury was for many in that community a torchbearer and, though he never came out formally, his biographer Lesley-Ann Jones spoke to those closest to him and they all said that 'Bohemian Rhapsody' was in fact his coming-out song. It is significant that it is one of the most popular and influential songs of the pop music era, as Mercury sings about the need to 'face the truth' and the anguish of living in denial for such a long time.

The post-modern narrative of 'Be whoever you want to be' is a more recent development. Many post-modern thinkers have rejected the idea, central to the modern story, that there is a fixed 'you' to be true to. Ultimately, they say, all identity is socially constructed and, therefore, 'you' are a blank slate, free to build your identity as you choose. This narrative is behind a lot of the experiences and identity expressions within the transgender community, though, as we will see in a moment, not all. So, if a person wants to dress as a man today then fine, but if he or she wants to be a woman tomorrow because his or her gender is fluid, then that is up to him or her too. The British comedian Eddie Izzard would go out on stage sometimes dressed as a man, sometimes dressed as a woman, often wearing an outfit that was a mixture of both. Eddie talked of having 'a boy mode and a girl mode' and switching between them (even though since 2020 the comedian has said, 'I just want to be based in girl mode from now on').[2] That's the 'Be whoever you want to be' attitude. Some prominent technologies reinforce this view: at the time of writing, Facebook has seventy-one gender options to choose from because many people see identity as fluid.

To make things a bit more complicated, not all trans people would identify with this 'Be whoever you want to be' narrative. Caitlyn Jenner is arguably one of the most famous transgender people alive today. When the former Olympic athlete and reality TV star came out as a woman in April 2015 and self-identified with the pronouns 'she' and 'her', she framed her personal journey as needing to be 'true to herself' (the modern narrative) and said in numerous interviews words to the effect of

In a simple way, there was always this woman that lived inside of me. But I lived my life as Bruce. But she was always there, she was always present. I just finally got to the point in life where it's time for her to live.[3]

Narratives in conflict

It is important to see that these two identity narratives are mutually exclusive. The modern narrative assumes that there is a 'you' that you need to find and be true to. Therefore, ultimately identity is fixed and is something to be discovered. The post-modern narrative assumes that there is ultimately no 'you', because identity is a blank canvas on which you can paint a hundred different 'selves'. When you pause and think about it, it can't be true both that there is ultimately a 'you' that you need to be true to, and that there is no 'you' because you are a blank canvas. In fact, post-modern thinkers are often overtly critical of the modern view of self for not going far enough. Their concern is that in seeking to be true to yourself you aren't yet fully free to be whoever you want to be.

Understanding that these two narratives are in conflict helps us to grasp many of the current culture wars about sexuality and gender. Very often the LGBT community is presented as one united whole, but is it? Stonewall is arguably the foremost LGBT lobbying group in the UK, but back in early 2019 it lost a large chunk of its supporters and its chief executive Ruth Hunt over this issue. Many gay and lesbian campaigners felt that the new trans agenda undermined what they had fought so hard for. After all, if someone has spent their life fighting for gay rights, but then a man who is heterosexual self-identifies as a woman, saying now that 'she' is a lesbian, then to what extent can that person really identify with the gay rights struggle? Or, if that is all too confusing, think of the way J. K. Rowling, a prominent supporter of women's and gay rights, refused to validate the term 'people who menstruate', instead saying that such a term simply described 'women'. Many in the trans community were outraged by this, saying that she was discriminating against those who were biologically male but self-identified as women. Daniel Radcliffe, who played Harry Potter in the films, made a public statement – which received considerable support – rebuking Rowling for her stance, claiming, 'Transgender women are women!' Some pointed out that while a key element of women's rights had been the right to be free from the patriarchy dictating terms to women, suddenly a white privileged male (Radcliffe) was telling a woman (Rowling) that she didn't know what it was to be one and subsequently being applauded by the culture for doing so. They felt aggrieved, since that was a key part of what the women's rights movement had campaigned to be free from. This resulted in a stand-off, with both sides angry and both sides pointing out the way the others were infringing on their minority rights. You can see the confusion that the crosswinds of these competing narratives create.

If you are finding all this rather confusing or difficult to follow, it is! And that is part of the point: when feelings are running high because something as essential as identity is at stake, disentangling competing narratives is painful and messy. It is indeed a moral maze. So how can we navigate a way forward?

What is behind the identity narratives?

To try to see a way forward, let us think about what the primary desires are behind these narratives. Behind both these identity projects are really two key desires: security and liberty. I would go as far as to say that these are two pillars that underpin every identity.

In traditional societies and many non-Western cultures, identity was (and is) largely fixed. Traditional identity is constituted by things outside ourselves, such as nationality, race, family, status and role.

These things are 'out there' and they determine our identity. Often our surnames, which date back to pre-modern times, give this away. If I am a 'Davidson', then my identity is determined by a man called David and my relationship to him. If David was a man with honour and status within the community that would be good, but if he was a person shunned by my community then that association would be shameful. Similarly, my identity might be linked to my job, so if I am a 'Smith' then that's a relatively menial role bashing metal, but if I am a 'Masterton' then I am the master of the town – a position of status and honour. The philosopher Charles Taylor describes such identities as 'porous' because of the way that these outside factors filter through and determine our 'selves'.[4] In being bound up with relatively fixed external factors, such identities were themselves pretty stable, which was good. But they were also very restrictive. What if I don't like being a 'Smith' and want to become something different; can I? What if I don't like my identity and find it very constraining: how do I change?

Christianity is often associated with a 'traditional' identity narrative and, therefore, it is assumed that it is constraining. The thought runs like this: religious people attach their identity to their religion, just as some people used to attach their identity to their nation. All such identity narratives have been shown to be constraining, so Christianity must be outdated and constraining. However, as we will see, this is an incorrect diagnosis. Christianity is not a call to find your identity by a religion or system of belief but an invitation to receive an identity from God. This is not, in any sense, a traditional identity narrative. It is a radically different identity narrative.

In response to the traditional narrative, modernity broke away from this and, rather than identity being tied to something outside ourselves, it became something to be discovered within ourselves. Charles Taylor calls this the 'buffered self' for the way that our identities resisted or buffered external factors and became about what lies within; hence the call to 'be true to yourself'. This was a move towards greater liberty, but the move brought a corresponding loss of security. Because, if I look within myself, to what extent do I really find a coherent and unchanging set of desires? We all are aware of how much our internal life is subject to change, and not just with regard to small things but with larger things too. That is why when people want to guarantee a commitment they 'secure' it by binding it to something external, for example by placing a hand on a Bible and 'swearing by Almighty God', or, in the case of a financial transaction, guaranteeing repayment by 'securing' it to a valuable item. If our intentions or commitments were secure in themselves, this practice would be redundant, but we all know they aren't.

Post-modern identity – 'Be whoever you want to be' – is a further move towards liberty but it is also a further move away from security. If I can be whoever I want to be, then it sounds wonderfully freeing. But, if there is ultimately no coherent or fixed me, isn't that also ultimately insecure? When all my achievements, choices and desires are stripped away, what is left? Am I really anything at all?

The challenge then is to have a liberating identity that is still secure and a secure identity that is still liberating. But is this achievable?

The failure of the identity narratives

Whichever of the narratives of identity particularly resonates with you, they all have something in common: they are all building identity on some*thing*. Traditional identities are built on something external. Modern identities are built on something discovered internally. Post-modern identities are built on our choices. And, as Jesus said in one of his more famous parables, whenever you are building on something it is important to see whether it can bear the weight or whether, when the storms of life come, it will crumble (Matthew 7:24–27).

What is the essence of who we are?

When it comes to identity, the Apostle Paul is a fascinating and complex character. He was a person who had every advantage in the ancient Middle-Eastern context. Honoured within Jewish society as a religious leader with an impeccable ethnic lineage, he was morally upright and devout. He was also (and unusually) a Roman citizen and therefore able to mix within Gentile circles. And his formidable intelligence and incredible work ethic are borne out by his writings and his impact on the world. As sources of identity go, he had a pretty impressive list to draw on.

His physical journey on the road to Damascus is well known, but the journey he had to take in reconstructing his identity is less well known but, for our purposes in this chapter, vitally important. In his letter to the Philippians he was writing to a celebrated Roman colony that enjoyed considerable kudos for giving its name to the largest Roman battle up to that point, at which (in 42 BC) Mark Antony and Octavian had gained revenge on Julius Caesar's assassins, Brutus and Cassius. Not only that, but Philippi was very wealthy because of its proximity to gold mines (it had its own coin mint) and because of its trade routes. For the people of that time, the temptation to find their identity in their status as 'Philippians' would be huge. But Paul wrote to warn them about the pitfalls of such an identity. A lesson he himself had learned.

First, he had come to realize the inadequacy of his sources of identity. He writes:

> But whatever [sources of identity] were gains to me I now con-
> sider loss . . . I consider them garbage, that I may gain Christ
> and be found in him.
> (Philippians 3:7–9)

The word 'garbage' is a particularly restrained translation; the original word literally means excrement! Paul is saying, in the strongest possible terms, that he has had to learn the lesson of the futility of seeking to construct identity on the basis of anything other than Christ. Why does he say this?

First, because nothing that we build our identity on in this world will be secure enough and, second, because nothing we can build our identity on in this world will be liberating enough.

Security

A constructed identity builds on external things such as family, career, nationality or popularity, or it is founded on internal things such as our sense of who we are, a desire for fulfilment or a need to be in control. But, whatever those things are, they are always transient. If you build your identity on your popularity then it may feel pretty solid when people are singing your praises, but what about when the crowd turns on you? You don't just experience a loss of your popularity; it actually amounts to a loss of identity. I used to work with professional sportspeople in my role at Christians in Sport, and the negative impact on their psyche of looking to the crowd for their sense of worth is well documented. Perform well and they are elated, but have a bad race or match and they die a thousand deaths. They can't stop thinking not only that they have just experienced a loss, but also that they are a loser. It wasn't just a bad game; they are a bad human being. Their performance becomes their core identity.

Or, if your identity is founded on a desire to be in control, what happens when life throws you a curve ball and things start to get untangled? It is not just that circumstances then feel in flux but that your very sense of who you are is destabilized. Anxiety sets in, followed by frenetic attempts to 'get back in control', all the while acknowledging the painful reality that, even if you can get things in order for a bit, it won't last long.

Not only this, but when we build our identity on something in this world, we have to deal with the great enemy of death. In Hebrew thinking, 'Sheol' was a place of cosmic darkness, where the things we value and treasure in this world dissipate (Job 7:9) and turn to dust (Psalm 103:14). A few years ago I was in Cairo and went to see the Tutankhamun exhibition. When Egyptian pharaohs died they were buried with precious items in the belief that they could take them with them and benefit from them in the afterlife. Tutankhamun had been buried with many of his 'treasures', for example his chariots – two large ceremonial ones, a smaller decorative one and three others for daily use. It just so happened that on the plane over to Egypt I had idly watched *MTV Cribs* (where viewers are shown the stunning homes and possessions of various household names) and seen a celebrity showing off his car collection! More than three thousand years separate Tutankhamun and that celebrity, but they had both made the same mistake, because death takes it all away: possessions, achievements, family, our very selves.

Liberty

The other problem with a constructed identity is that whatever it is that we are building our sense of self on will enslave us. C. S. Lewis memorably writes about this in *Mere Christianity*:

> Most people, if they have really learned to look into their own hearts, would know that they do want, and want acutely, something that cannot be had in this world. There are all sorts of things in this world that offer to give it to you, but they never quite keep their promise. The longings which arise in us when we first fall in love, or first think of some foreign country, or first take up some subject that excites us, are longings which no marriage, no travel, no learning, can really satisfy.[5]

The disjunction between our longings and the actual experience creates a kind of enslavement. Some 'chase the high', thinking that if only they could experience *more* of what they are pursuing, they will be satisfied. Others become disillusioned and think that they just need to find something *better* or more satisfying, and so swap one identity source for another, not realizing that they are destined to go through the same experience over and over again. The tragic irony is that each of our sources of identity carries with it the whispered promise of freedom but produces only slavery.

On one level we should know this, because the warnings have been written in a hundred books, parables and songs throughout the ages. Sirens seducing sailors towards shipwreck and ruin. Hansel and Gretel lured to a gingerbread house in a wood and then being trapped by a witch. King Midas lusting for the golden touch only for tragedy to strike as he turns into gold first his daughter and then the river, and so dies of despair and thirst. The warning signs are there, but of course that's the greatest irony of all: we think, 'I will be different; I will find the security and liberation that have evaded countless others', not realizing that no constructed identity can ever be secure enough or liberating enough for us.

Receiving a secure and liberating identity

If, first of all, the Apostle Paul had to learn the inadequacy of the sources of our identity, the second step was that he had to receive his identity *in Christ*:

> What is more, I consider everything a loss because of the surpassing worth of knowing Christ Jesus my Lord, for whose sake I have lost all things. I consider them garbage, that I may gain Christ and be found in him, not having a righteousness of my own that comes from the law, but that which is through

faith in Christ – the righteousness that comes from God on the basis of faith.
(Philippians 3:8–9)

Notice how Paul is contrasting the sources of his identity, considered now as 'garbage', with gaining Christ. He is not saying that the things, in and of themselves, are rubbish. Far from it: the better something is, the more likely we are to want to build the architecture of our lives on it. But, in comparison with Christ, Paul considers them nothing. Why is that? Because, he says, he does not have to achieve righteousness by works of the law, but can receive righteousness through faith in Christ.

The word 'righteousness' here initially sounds like a peculiarly religious concept, removed from day-to-day life. But it is actually a word that is sometimes translated 'justification', and that, for me, feels more intuitive. How often do we feel the pressure to 'justify' ourselves, our actions or our choices? One of my favourite films is David Puttnam's 1981 historical drama *Chariots of Fire*. The film centres on the comparison between two great Olympians, Harold Abrahams and Eric Liddell. Both competed at the 1924 Paris Olympics, Abrahams in the 100 metres and Liddell, famously, in the 400 metres. In the film, before the 100 metres final, Abrahams is in the changing room with his friend Aubrey and he says:

> You, Aubrey, are my most complete man. You're brave, compassionate, kind: a content man. That is your secret, contentment; I am 24 and I've never known it. I'm forever in pursuit and I don't even know what I am chasing. And now in one hour's time I will be out there again. I will raise my eyes and look down that corridor; 4 feet wide, with 10 lonely seconds to justify my whole existence. But will I?

Abrahams is facing the pressure and enslavement of a constructed identity. In contrast, Eric Liddell is a Christian, and he says the simple but profound words, 'When I run, I feel God's pleasure.'

The great difference portrayed between the two is that, for Abrahams, his running is, as he calls it, an addiction. It is something he craves for what it can give him as regards his identity. His whole life is about his longing to achieve enough, to be enough, to feel justified. In contrast, Liddell as a Christian has received his identity in Christ – by faith. He has received justification from God and therefore has no need to justify himself. His running is a gift to be enjoyed rather than an edifice on which to build his identity. This means that he can take it for what it is, a good thing, but that it does not define him.

What does it mean to receive justification by faith? To be justified first of all means to know that Christ has died for all of the ways that we construct our identity independently of God. Scripture tells us that we are God's masterpieces, uniquely bearing his image, which makes each one of us, regardless of gender, race, background, life experiences, achievements or the appraisal of others, inestimably valuable. But rather than receive our identity as God's image bearers we have chosen to construct our identity on good things that God has created. This is both deeply offensive to God and also ultimately foolish. The crushing insecurity and enslavement we experience are part of the just consequences and judgment from God for that decision.

But when Jesus Christ dies on the cross, he takes the judgment that we deserve. For those who seek their identity in success, Jesus became a cosmic failure on the cross for their sake. For those who seek their identity in popularity, Jesus was despised and rejected, with God the Father ultimately turning his back on him. For those who look within themselves for their identity, Jesus experienced the supreme anguish and inner turmoil of being forsaken by his Father as he cried out, 'My God, my God, why have you forsaken me?' He took all of this, so that he might pay for the ways we have sought to construct our lives independently of the one who made us and loves us.

Second, the cross shows us how loved we are. We all want to be loved, but because we know we are flawed we fear that if we remove all the masks and show someone 'the real me', they won't love us. Consequently, we never really show someone 'me', warts and all. We hide behind filters, online profiles, make-up and projections of ourselves. But if we never really let anyone see the real me, then no one will ever really love the real me. Surely there is no greater tragedy than going through life never being really loved.

But when Jesus dies on the cross he is dying for you, the real you, the you behind a hundred masks, the you that you fear revealing. And because he sees you, failures and all, and at that moment dies for you, you can truly know that you are loved. More than this, because his love is given to you not because of anything you have done but as a free gift, it can never be taken away. To be loved for who you really are is liberating; to be loved in such a way that it can never be taken away provides true security. That is why Paul says that this 'righteousness that comes from God' is such good news! This is why he says it is the one thing that is to be considered valuable above all other things. Because, in a powerfully profound way, it is the one thing that enables us to experience and value anything else without making it into a source of our identity.

Francis Thompson was a Victorian poet who, feeling the burden of living up to his family's expectations, turned instead to opium and became addicted. It is a familiar tale of fractured identity. He would sleep rough in London around Charing Cross and the River Thames, occasionally penning poems that made even critics describe him as

'finer than any poet since Shakespeare'. One night, on the banks of
the Thames, he had an intense conversion experience that led him to
Christ and eventually his rehabilitation. Through his circumstances
he perceived God pursuing him, beating 'at his own clay-shuttered
doors', trying to bring him to the end of his striving for an identity
in achievements, a path that had led to his ruin, and instead urging
him to receive his identity as a free gift. This is the poem he wrote
about that night. As you read it, why not let the words prompt you
to reflect on your own story, what you are seeking to build your
identity on, and what it might look like if your identity was in Christ.

In no strange land

O world invisible, we view thee,
O world intangible, we touch thee,
O world unknowable, we know thee,
Inapprehensible, we clutch thee!

Does the fish soar to find the ocean,
The eagle plunge to find the air–
That we ask of the stars in motion
If they have rumour of thee there?

Not where the wheeling systems darken,
And our benumbed conceiving soars!–
The drift of pinions, would we hearken,
Beats at our own clay-shuttered doors.

The angels keep their ancient places–
Turn but a stone and start a wing!
'Tis ye, 'tis your estrangèd faces,
That miss the many-splendoured thing.

What is the essence of who we are?

But (when so sad thou canst not sadder)
Cry;–and upon thy so sore loss
Shall shine the traffic of Jacob's ladder
Pitched betwixt Heaven and Charing Cross.

Yea, in the night, my Soul, my daughter,
Cry,–clinging to Heaven by the hems;
And lo, Christ walking on the water,
Not of Genesareth, but Thames![6]

Hope is a bit like
your keys: if you put
it in the wrong place,
you will lose it.

6

Hope

What does the future hold?

Hope versus optimism

My wife set a record for being the latest bride ever at the church where we got married in central London. Some of my friends have teased me that they could understand why she would pause for thought! I remember it vividly: a church full of people, everyone sitting down expecting the bride to arrive any time soon; fifteen minutes late, twenty-five minutes late, thirty minutes late! I could sense the mood in the church change at some point. The normal buzz of conversation had been replaced by hushed and concerned tones. 'Do you think she's coming?' 'I'm sure there's a good reason she's so late.' 'But what if . . . You don't think . . . ?' Up to that point I had been optimistic that Rebecca would not leave me in the lurch. Then one of my groomsmen hurried towards me at the front of the church. He'd had a phone call from someone in the bridal car; they were on their way, stuck in bad traffic (that's London for you). Now I had hope! Rebecca did eventually arrive, only forty-five minutes late.

One of the challenges when we explore the idea of hope is the limitation of the English language. The New Testament is written in Greek, and it is a wonderfully precise language. English is a bit more approximate. In Greek there are two main words for 'hope': *thelo*, which is a general expression of desire akin to optimism, and *elpizo*, which is hope with a reasonable expectation of fulfilment. In this chapter we are not so much considering whether we are glass-half-empty or glass-half-full people, we are thinking about hope in the *elpizo* sense; you could call it 'sure hope'.

Hope is fundamental to life

We might be tempted to think that hope is something we need only when life gets tough; a sort of 'break glass in case of emergency' virtue. But hope is incredibly important for all of life. Hope is about looking forward, seeing a different and better situation or world. Richard Bauckham writes, in his book *Hope Against Hope*:

> Hope is among those capacities or activities which mark off the territory of the distinctively human within our world. The quest for meaning, truth, goodness and beauty is closely bound up with hope as an activity of imagination in which we seek to transcend the boundaries of the present, to go beyond the given, outwards and forward, in search of something more, something better, than the given affords us ... Hope is born the moment we believe that the good things we wish for and imagine having are possible for us to have.[1]

What he is saying is that hope is fundamental for all human activities. Think of morality and discussions of how we should live: hope enables us to look at the current situation and then imagine a future that could or should be different. That is why morality is always framed within a narrative of where we have come from and where we are going, and then, in the light of that, of how we should act. It is an exercise in hope. Or think about art: in 1982, in the catalogue text for the documenta 7 exhibition, the abstract artist and giant of the modern art movement Gerhard Richter said, 'Art is the highest form of hope.' Art is about cultivating a sense of the 'ideal' and moving forward towards that by creating new possibilities. That's hope. Similarly, technological innovation is bound up with hope. We see this in the way that software updates are often labelled by progressing numbers. Currently I'm using Mac OS 10.13.6. It is almost redundant to ask if OS 8 is worse or better than OS 10, because we just all assume that the latest updates are better as we move forward towards a goal of technological improvement. That is hope.

To give a sense of how essential hope is to life, a seminal study was conducted by the Joseph Rowntree Foundation into the impact of allowing residents of care homes to keep pets. The study noticed that focusing on the pets gave the residents hope, and the results were quite remarkable. Those with pets had a lower risk of heart attack and stroke and were less likely to develop heart failure. They typically spent 30% less time in hospital, required 15% fewer GP visits and took fewer prescription medications. If there was a drug that could provide similar results it would be considered near miraculous! That's the power of hope.[2]

Hope is fundamental to facing death

Hope is also fundamental to facing death. In the West there has been a steady and concerted disengagement from death. It has often been commented that whereas the Victorians were prudish and repressed any talk of sex but were remarkably open in talking about death, today the positions have been reversed. We are very open when talking about sex but repress any talk of death. It is hard to overstate just how strange this is, particularly when you consider the certainty of death. As a pastor I take funerals, and one of the funeral directors I work with always says goodbye the same way: 'See you next time!' That is the certainty of death. How strange to spend our lives seeking to avoid the unavoidable. But it is not just strange; it is also an anomaly when we compare the West with other cultures. In fact, I would go as far as to say that the West today is the only culture that is not prepared to face death.

Go back just a hundred years and a third of all children would die before their fifth birthday. It was normal if you were planning a family to factor this in. Just imagine that conversation and how it would normalize death, particularly when most of those deaths would happen in your home. Similarly, other cultures today are explicitly shaped by death. Some have a huge focus on ancestors and ancestral worship because they believe you live on through your family. Traditional African and some Latin American cultures see a thin filter between the physical world and the spiritual realm, where spirits live on after death. Hindu cultures teach reincarnation as the means by which the souls of those who die carry on. Buddhist cultures teach that death is part of the veil of suffering, an illusion one can pass through into Nirvana. What all of these cultures have in common is that they have an explicit way of thinking about the world that seeks to face up to and deal with death. Hope is therefore crucial to these cultures. As Andrew Delbanco comments:

> The heart of any culture is hope, hope is the way we overcome the lurking suspicion that all our getting and spending amounts to nothing more than fidgeting while we wait for death. We must imagine some end to life that transcends our own tiny allotment of days and hours if we are to keep at bay the dim, back-of-the-mind suspicion that one may be adrift in an absurd world.[3]

But in the West our secular framing of life means that there is no supernatural, no soul to live on, no afterlife; this life is all there is. Therefore, how do we 'overcome the lurking suspicion that all our getting and spending amounts to fidgeting while we wait for death'? The truth is we either expend a great deal of energy seeking to avoid death or surround it with vague but well-meaning platitudes that lack any real substance of hope.

During the months of the COVID pandemic, it was starkly evident that suddenly every day we were being confronted with death. News reports pored over the pandemic curve and countries were constantly compared on the basis of their daily death toll. The result for a culture unprepared to stare death in the face was traumatizing. Our normal refuges of medicine and science were being looked to but had few answers in the early stages. My wife is a surgeon and was working in the central London hospital that dealt with more infectious cases than any other. Initially it seemed that only the elderly and those with underlying health conditions were at risk, but when a seemingly healthy man in his mid twenties died a few weeks in, a number of her colleagues (who are normally a pretty sanguine bunch) started breaking down emotionally, fearing that they too might die. She had numerous conversations with them in which they asked her why she seemed so calm, given that all their lives were at risk. The focus of those conversations quickly became her hope as a Christian to be able to face death without fear. Not how to avoid it, not how to sentimentalize it with wishful-thinking optimism, but how to face it with realism and yet hope. Hope is fundamental to facing death.

How have we lost hope?

Hope is a bit like your keys: if you put it in the wrong place, you will lose it. As we have been seeing, hope is essential to life and death, and therefore strictly speaking everyone has hope. Those whom we sometimes might describe as being 'hopeless' are not people who have tried to live without hope, but those who have put their hope in the wrong place and have lost it. I think that one of the defining features of our culture is that we have lost hope by putting it in the wrong place.

Part of the way that this can be observed is in the shrinking horizon as we look to the future. When we feel confident about the future, we make long-term plans and the horizon stretches out before us.

We 'invest' in the future. When we feel the future is uncertain, it becomes more risky to invest in it and therefore we become more focused on the here and now. The horizon shrinks and comes nearer to the present. This is true not only in financial investments but in general terms as well.

One of the ways we see this in the West is in our embracing of nostalgia. If looking to the future becomes unattractive or uncertain then we focus on the here and now. We long for the home of yesteryear. That's what 'nostalgia' means: in Greek, *nostos* is a return home and *algos* pain or longing. Think of the way that over the past couple of decades retro fashion trends and fads have become so popular. Think of the reruns and rehashes of childhood films and TV series such as *Ghostbusters* and *Star Wars*; even the rise of superhero films and the Marvel and DC 'universes' hark back to the childhood comics they originated from. Think of the surge in demand for vinyl, increasing by 30% in 2015 despite the success of Spotify. The retro/nostalgia cultural movement is hugely popular.

And nostalgia is not just important at the level of popular culture. It is a key part of some of the most influential political trends of our time. Donald Trump justified his nationalist and protectionist measures with the slogan 'Make America great again'. Notice the nostalgic emphasis on 'again'. Similarly, the Chinese president Xi Jinping, in the same period, called for 'a great *rejuvenation* of the Chinese people' (my emphasis). In the same way, Russia has been seeking to 'regain' its prominence in the world and Japan has been looking back to the Meiji restoration of the nineteenth century from which it expanded its empire. Nostalgia is a powerful political and cultural dynamic because when the future looks uncertain we tend to focus on the here and now and long for the security of yesteryear.

But why is the future so uncertain? It is all about where we are placing our hope. Like keys, we have put our hope in the wrong place and so we have lost it. One of the important ideological changes that happened in the Enlightenment was that we relocated our hope. I have already suggested that the Enlightenment was a rejection of the idea of God, in part because of failures within the institutional church and in part because of the corresponding rise of 'the age of reason'. So, in the West, we shifted our hope from God and the church, and we put our hope in humanity. The post-Enlightenment period was to be the humanist period. Here is the second Humanist Manifesto from 1973:

> The next century can be and should be the humanistic century. Dramatic scientific, technological, and ever-accelerating social and political changes crowd our awareness. We have virtually conquered the planet, explored the moon, overcome the natural limits of travel and communication; we stand at the dawn of a new age, ready to move farther into space and perhaps inhabit other planets. Using technology wisely, we can control our environment, conquer poverty, markedly reduce disease, extend our life-span, significantly modify our behavior, alter the course of human evolution and cultural development, unlock vast new powers, and provide humankind with unparalleled opportunity for achieving an abundant and meaningful life.[4]

The problem is that, despite real and important advances in many areas of our society, there have also been significant setbacks that have eroded this humanist hope. It is difficult now to fully grasp just what optimism accompanied the dawn of the twentieth century, but many in the West really thought that it would be a period to bring in the second Humanist Manifesto's aspirations. In Paris in 1900 there was an international exposition, showing more than 80,000 exhibits from forty countries and attended by more than 40 million people (at a time when long-distance travel was not straightforward). Its purpose: to show-case the achievements of the nineteenth century and to accelerate development into the twentieth century.

But from 1914 the twentieth century was a period of almost unbroken war. It was the bloodiest period in history, with somewhere between 150 and 240 million people dying in conflict and few and brief periods of relative peace. Of course there were important advances in science and technology, and real improvements in many areas such as education and health, but it is difficult to overstate just what a hammer blow this period was to the narrative of 'hope in humanity'. Not only this, but even when we have enjoyed times of relative peace and prosperity, as we saw in the chapter on happiness, the advances in technology and improvements in quality of life have not led to the sense of psychological well-being that we would have expected.

As a result, we find ourselves today longing for hope but deeply sceptical about those who promise it. For example, it is difficult to think of a better example of a politician in North America who tried to leverage hope than Barack Obama. And yet, even for his election campaign in 2008, there had to be a significant downplaying of hope for his candidacy to be plausible. Initially his campaign led with the slogan 'Change you can believe in'; a hope-filled message of real change. Despite his skills as an orator and the waves of enthusiasm that would lead him to victory, feedback from polling surveys quickly showed that this message was met with scepticism on the part of voters. So it was downgraded to 'The change we need'. This was effectively saying the minimum amount of hope the electorate would stomach!

I wonder whether on a personal level you identify with this loss of hope. I spend quite a lot of time working with Millennials and one of the consistent themes I hear from them is that they feel trapped. On one level they are told, 'The world is your oyster; you will be the generation to change the world.' They feel that a significant weight of hope is being placed on their shoulders. But on the other hand they are faced with some very challenging realities. Unprecedented levels of student debt, sky-high house prices (particularly in leading cities) that mean home owning is a distant reality for most, difficulty getting a job after education, increasing awareness of big problems in the world such as racism and climate change. This tension between people putting their hope in them and their feeling that they are struggling just to get by creates significant dissonance and anxiety. There is a longing for hope but also a realization of how much pressure it puts on someone when we make them the one who has to carry the burden of our expectations. This is a key part of the Enlightenment's legacy and our loss of hope.

Putting hope in the right place

Hope is a ship that has to sail between two rocks, naivety and cynicism. Naivety will shipwreck hope by causing us to trust in something that will only let us down. On the other hand, cynicism shipwrecks hope by saying that because you have misplaced it in the past, you will never find something or someone who is trustworthy in the future.

We often see these twin challenges of naivety and cynicism in our approach to relationships. Some people are too naive and trusting. They keep putting their hope in the wrong person and end up getting taken for a ride. Others, sadly often because they have been let down in the past, hold back from commitment and become increasingly cynical. The real tragedy is that both approaches lead to a damaged heart. Naivety damages your heart by leaving it unguarded and exposed such that it becomes wounded by successive let-downs. Cynicism damages your heart by locking it away behind the bars of self-preservation and caution where it becomes increasingly hardened and brittle. But there is an alternative, a course that navigates us safely past naivety and cynicism. We have to put hope in the right place.

The early Christians were distinguished by their hope. For the majority, to become a Christian in the ancient world was to make your life substantially harder. There were periods of state-led persecution when Christians were imprisoned, had their belongings confiscated or were publicly executed, such as under Emperors Nero (after AD 64) and Domitian (AD 81–96), when infamously Christians were fed to lions in the public arena. But even when persecution wasn't state-led, for the most part of the first 300 years of the church, Christians were rejected by society at large and treated with no small measure of scorn. In an honour–shame culture, to follow one whose symbol – the cross – was an instrument of torture for common criminals was deeply shameful. And yet, under these conditions, the church did not just endure but it thrived. At the end of the first century there were fewer than 10,000 Christians in the Roman Empire. By the end of the second century this had increased to about 200,000 Christians; by the year AD 250 this was about a million and by the year AD 300 Christians made up nearly 10% of the population (about 6 million).[5]

What accounts for this remarkable growth? One crucial factor is the distinctiveness of Christian hope, located as it was in Jesus' resurrection from the dead. A hope that avoids the dangers of naivety and cynicism in at least three important ways: by engaging with reality, by being historically true and by being full of wonder. Let's consider these one by one.

Avoiding naivety by engaging with reality

The starting point of the resurrection is not actually Easter Sunday but Good Friday, just as the starting point of hope lies in an engagement with the difficult realities of the world and supremely with death.

One of the things we struggle with is that on the one hand death is so universal as to be arguably the most normal thing there is, and on the other hand everything about death feels abnormal. In his 1947 poem 'Do Not Go Gentle into That Good Night', Dylan Thomas famously highlighted the way that we rage against death because of our profound sense that it should not be this way. But, of course, it is. How do we account for this? Jesus' death makes sense of our intuition because the explanation for death does not lie in naturalism, nor is it just the inevitable result of entropy; rather, death is the tragic consequence of our rejection of God.

Jesus' death on that first Good Friday shows us this rejection in its full ugliness. Despite his innocence, despite his unparalleled life of love, some, such as Judas and the religious leaders, actively plotted Jesus' death. Some, such as the Roman governor, Pilate, cared more about their political career and 'keeping the peace' than about doing the right thing, and thereby enabled Jesus' death. Others got caught up with the crowd calling for Jesus' death and the release of the criminal Barabbas, merely because everyone else was doing it and they lacked the moral courage to stand against the majority. Is this not starkly realistic? One can look at almost any moment of collective evil in human history and see the same dynamics. Think, for example, of the Holocaust. Some deliberately sought to bring it about, many others enabled it through their weakness and inability to act justly, still many others went along with the crowd and did what everyone else was doing. In the same way, on an individual level, isn't it true that many of our failures to be the people we should be, the people God wants us to be, are bound up with these dynamics?

Jesus' death, then, is an exposé of evil, showing that it really exists, not 'out there' in some different class of person, but, as Solzhenitsyn famously wrote, cutting right through the heart of every human being.[6] The starting point of Christian hope is starkly realistic. This shows us why the humanism of the post-Enlightenment period was always a poor place to put our hope. Ultimately, it was too naive about human nature and failed to reckon with sin. Its dreams were always destined to be dashed on the rocks of reality. We should not have needed two world wars to show us that.

But Jesus' death is also God's assessment of and judgment on evil. We instinctively feel that death shouldn't be this way, and the cross shows us where this comes from. God made a world of life and love, but when we turn away from him who is the source of all life then we are implicitly choosing death. God treats us as morally responsible agents and so his judgment is to give us over to the consequences of this decision: physical death and after that eternal existence in a terrible lived reality the Bible calls hell. The cross affirms our deep intuition that death is profoundly abnormal despite its ubiquity. We die because of how we (fail to) respond to God, and we see that beyond all doubt at the cross. Jesus, the source of all life and goodness, is rejected by those he made and loved, and God will judge us for this. Even though the majority of us weren't there, the cross exposes what lies in every human heart and is played out in the day-to-day rejection of God in each of our lives. The cross also shows us what God, as the perfectly just Creator, must do in response.

Once again, here is no sugar-coated, two-dimensional escapism. Instead, the Christian hope confronts the worst: sin, evil, death. These are the dark realities through which the Christian hope shines brightest. I hope you can see that there is no sense in which Christianity is naive. Nothing could be further from the truth; it is starkly realistic about what we are really like, the existence of evil in the world and the ultimate tragedy of death.

Avoiding naivety by historical truth

It is not just that the Christian hope is realistic; it is also true – taking place in space, time and history. Because many people do not read the Bible for themselves, they often miss just how historically rooted the resurrection accounts are. In Luke's account we are told:

> On the first day of the week, very early in the morning, the women took the spices they had prepared and went to the tomb. (Luke 24:1)

There are a number of things to notice from this. First, it is the women who are going to Jesus' tomb. The men, the remaining eleven disciples (after the betrayal of Judas), are nowhere to be seen. They are frightened and bewildered, hiding behind locked doors, fearing for their lives because their leader has been brutally executed. When Jesus died their hopes lay in tatters. The hope that the disciples came to embrace, the hope that meant they were willing to be martyred, proclaiming the resurrection to their dying breath, was not something that was innate to them as 'religious' or 'courageous' people. Their starting point was despair and desolation; they were moral cowards until the hope of the resurrection broke in.

Second, the significance of the women going to the tomb is that this made them the first eyewitnesses to Jesus' resurrection (see, for example, Matthew 28:1–10). In a traditional patriarchal society like theirs, neither in a Roman nor in a Jewish court of law was women's testimony considered valid unless corroborated by men. So, if this was a fabricated account, why would women be the key eyewitnesses? Send Peter, James and John, bold and full of hope, expecting to greet the risen Jesus. But don't send a small and frightened band of women whose testimony would not initially be believed even by the disciples themselves! The resurrection account is replete with the awkward realities of truth. Women at the tomb, men cowering behind closed doors, bewilderment rather than certainty, and fear rather than faith. It reads like history because it is.

But these trembling, bewildered people were soon to become bold witnesses. Paul's first letter to the church in Corinth is widely accepted, by secular and Christian historians alike, to have been written about twenty years or so after Jesus' death. In it Paul writes:

> For what I received I passed on to you as of first importance: that Christ died for our sins according to the Scriptures, that he was buried, that he was raised on the third day according to the Scriptures, and that he appeared to Cephas, and then to the Twelve. After that, he appeared to more than five hundred of the brothers and sisters at the same time, most of whom are still living, though some have fallen asleep. Then he appeared to James, then to all the apostles, and last of all he appeared to me also, as to one abnormally born.
>
> (1 Corinthians 15:3–8)

Keep it in mind that this was demonstrably a public document that was expected to be read out loud, copied and shared, and was in wide circulation not just in Corinth but throughout the region within twenty or so years of the events it is reporting. The challenge then for the sceptic is the ease with which the claims here could have been tested and proved false. Did Jesus really repeatedly appear in bodily resurrected form to hundreds of witnesses over a period of weeks? Ask them, since most would have been alive and in the church. It is hardly likely to be something that went unremarked! If he didn't, then surely these claims would have been quickly dismissed at source, as a fabrication. Equally, why, if the Apostles were making this up, did they make it so specific and concrete? Every child who has told a fib knows the basic rules of the lie: enough truth to make it plausible but sufficient vagueness to make it non-verifiable. Why

114

not then proclaim a 'spiritual' resurrection? That is much more vague and harder to verify. Why not say that Jesus appeared to only a select few? Who can test a private spiritual experience? Why not say that his resurrection appearances happened in some far-off place? But don't make it physical, public and local because then you make it verifiable. Unless, of course, it was.

Some say that people back then were just more gullible and prone to believing such fantasies. Well, perhaps it is true that today secularists are predisposed not to believe in miracles, but the early converts who believed in the resurrection were Jews and they were about the last people to accept the idea that God would become a man. God was so transcendent and holy in their view that they wouldn't even speak his name. The very idea that God would become man was considered blasphemy and punishable by death. Sceptics in the West may not like talk of the miraculous, but I have yet to have anyone try to stone me to death for it. But the Jews who didn't believe (as Paul initially didn't) viciously persecuted Christians for blasphemy. So what accounts for large numbers of these very people coming to believe that God became man, died on a cross and rose three days later in physical form, never to die again?

Often truth is stranger than fiction because we can't shape it to fit our preconceived ideas. So it is with the truth of the resurrection. It is stubbornly situated in space, time and history, defying sceptics, challenging presumptions and persuading unlikely believers that it really is true.

Avoiding cynicism by wonder

The above two points argue for the reality and historicity of Christian hope, which defend it against a charge of naivety, but how do we deal with the danger of cynicism? After all, aren't most people who are realistic and truthful also a little cynical? And yet the resurrection changed people such that they became starkly realistic about the world, passionately committed to truth and yet overflowing with joy and wonder. In Luke's Gospel, after the first resurrection appearance, he records two disciples on the road to Emmaus saying, 'Were not our hearts burning within us while he talked with us on the road and opened the Scriptures to us?' (Luke 24:32). Peter, the first disciple to witness Jesus' resurrection, writes in his first letter of an 'inexpressible and glorious joy' (1 Peter 1:8) that comes from believing in the risen Jesus.

And we can see why the resurrection leads to such wonder and joy when we consider its implications:

- If Jesus has risen from the dead, never to die again, then that means death is not the end. There is an eternity that is open to all who trust in him. Life beyond the grave is as certain as Jesus' resurrection from the grave (1 Corinthians 15:12 ff.).
- Not only that, but because death is the punishment for our rejection of God, when Jesus rises from the dead he shows us that the judgment has been completed. Just as a prisoner knows he has served his sentence when the doors of the prison are opened, so Jesus shows us that the sentence has been served because the grave opened its doors and Jesus walked out a free man. Our consciences can be clear, our guilt is paid for and we can be sure we are restored into a loving relationship with God because of Jesus' resurrection (Romans 4:25).
- The resurrection also shows us the reality that 'all things will be redeemed. Jesus' bodily resurrection is the 'firstfruits' of the renewal of all things (1 Corinthians 15:23). It is an agricultural metaphor. When the grape harvest is ready, the vineyard owner doesn't have to taste all the grapes to know this, just a representative sample. If the first fruits are ready then the whole harvest is. Jesus' resurrection is the first fruits of the

renewal of this whole world. The Christian hope is not some disembodied 'spiritual' existence but this world made new, renewed selves, a renewed creation. 'No more death or mourning or crying or pain, for the old order of things has passed away' (Revelation 21:4).

These are the implications of Jesus' resurrection that inspire such wonder and joy: death defeated, relationship with God restored for eternity and this world redeemed and renewed so that nothing bad will ever spoil it again.

I love reading stories to my children. I particularly love fairy stories, because of the children's reactions. The moment when Sleeping Beauty wakes up, or when the Beast becomes a prince and all his courtiers are restored. As I read, my children's eyes become as wide as the moon and they say to me, 'Daddy, is it true? Do people live happily ever after?' How should I answer? How would you?

J. R. R. Tolkien was not just one of the finest storytellers of the past century; he was also a professor of English language and literature. It was common in the post-war period for literary critics to take issue with the mythical and unhistorical. As a result, Tolkien gave a lesser-known lecture that was turned into a long essay defending fairy stories.[7] In it he argued that fairy stories are important because they deal with key themes that we need to engage with, principally: recovery, escapism and consolation.

- *Recovery* – recovering a true sense of the way things are, a 'cleaning of the windows' so that we see the world rightly.
- *Escapism* – not in the sense of disengaging with reality, but in the sense of validating our deep sense that there are things

in this world that we should seek to escape from: hunger, thirst, poverty, pain, sorrow, injustice, death.

- *Consolation* – meaning the deep and profound comfort of the 'Happy Ending'.

Unpacking the consolation of fairy stories, Tolkien talked about what he called 'the good catastrophe'. A catastrophe in literature technically means a sudden turn of events. So Tolkien was referring to the way in which there is a sudden turn in fairy stories, which leads to restoration. This is the bit we love in the great stories, the part where the heart quickens, children's eyes grow wide and, as Tolkien describes it, we are given 'a fleeting glimpse of joy'.

Tolkien goes on to say that in Christianity the great fairy story has entered into history and our world. The incarnation of Jesus Christ is the good catastrophe of humanity's history and the resurrection is the good catastrophe of the incarnation. It is the moment when (to use Tolkien's memorable phrase) everything sad really does come untrue. Therefore, it is not just a *glimpse* of joy, as in the fairy stories, but the true joy from which all fairy stories draw their power. Because of the resurrection we recover a true sense of the way the world should be, of the way the world will one day be. Because of the resurrection we realize the things that are wrong in the world that ultimately we need to escape from. Disease, depression, despair and death are not just the way things are; they are impostors who will one day be banished from the land. Because of the resurrection there is the deepest consolation of knowing that, one day, good will defeat evil, love will overcome hate and life will triumph over death.

So when my children turn to me with eyes wide open and ask, 'Daddy, is it true? Is there a happy ever after?', what do I say? What would you? Because of the resurrection of Jesus Christ and the real, true and wonderful hope that it provides, I don't have to default to fantasy and tell them a white lie so that they go to sleep untroubled. Nor do I merely have to educate them about the 'harsh realities' of life so that they don't end up being naive. Instead, I say to them, 'Is it true? Well, this is just a story, but you know in the true story about Jesus he really did rise from the dead and so, yes, there really is a happy ever after.'

The truth and attractiveness of Christianity is ultimately the truth and attractiveness of Jesus Christ himself.

God seeks those who are lost, who have lost the central importance of him in their lives, because he thinks it is worth the risk, because you are worth the risk.

Conclusion

A road back to God

This is water

In a speech to the 2005 graduating class of Kenyon College, Ohio, the late author David Foster Wallace told a parable that tapped into the way many in this generation are feeling. Two fish are in the sea swimming along, and coming the other way is an older fish. He greets them, saying, 'Morning, boys; how's the water?' The younger fish swim along a bit and then one turns to the other and says, 'What the hell is water?'

Wallace always had a knack of dialling into the disquiet of a generation aware of its own short-sightedness. He went on to elaborate:

> The point of the fish story is that the most obvious, important realities are often the ones that are hardest to see and talk about ... The fact is that in the day to day trenches of adult existence, banal platitudes can have a life or death importance.

Then, as he came to the end of his speech, he concluded:

> The capital-T Truth is about life BEFORE death. It is about the real value of a real education which has almost nothing to do with knowledge, and everything to do with simple awareness; awareness of what is so real and essential, so hidden in plain sight all around us, all the time, that we have to keep reminding ourselves over and over: This is water. This is water.[1]

In the same way, in this book I have been seeking to help us to become more attentive to the water we swim in. The ideas we hold, the beliefs we cherish and the narratives we tell hide in plain sight. They are everywhere around us but seldom considered. They shape our lives in countless ways but are rarely examined.

One way of thinking about this is to consider what we mean by 'faith'. Often faith is framed as a peculiar preserve of the religious. Frequently people who view themselves as 'not religious' will say to me words to the effect of 'I wish I had your faith'. I have pondered what they mean by this. At best, I think they are saying that they recognize that 'my faith' provides certain emotional resources that help me, and they find that attractive. But I am also aware of the popular definition of faith, which is 'believing things in spite of evidence to the contrary', and so I wonder if they are really saying, 'You believe in things that are not true, but at least you seem to be happy about it. In fact, you are so happy in your mild delusion that I actually find it attractive! But, try as I might, I'm just too rational and I can't make myself do it!!'

I'm obviously being playful with the analysis, but I don't think I'm far off the mark. Foster Wallace, however, would say that we all have faith. That is, we all swim in water. In fact, as I have already written, in the Bible faith is never seen as believing something in spite of evidence but as a response to evidence. The point is that you can't operate in life without a baseline set of assumptions about the way the world is.

Listen to the philosopher Martin Heidegger on this:

> I would say that men, for example Communists, have a reli-
> gion when they believe in science. They believe absolutely
> in modern science. And this is absolutely faith, that is, trust in

the certainty of the results of science, is a faith, and is, in a certain sense, something that emanates from people, and is therefore a religion.'[2]

Or here is the author Tom Holland:

So, essentially, what has happened is that I have lost my faith, and my faith was liberalism. I just don't think it has any secure foundations at all.[3]

Truth and beauty

Part of the significance of this analysis is that there is no such thing as being neutral. Often when people look into the claims of Jesus Christ they consider themselves to be in a neutral position, considering whether to 'make a commitment'. But that's not accurate. Instead, every person is already committed to a position. What I have been aiming to do is to help you evaluate your own commitments as you also evaluate what a life committed to Jesus Christ looks like.

As we have been going through the chapters I have been exploring our commitments from two particular standpoints: first, from a perspective of truth, considering the intellectual integrity of the viewpoint, and, second, from a perspective of beauty, considering the attractiveness of the viewpoint.

Truth is important because it is the hard edge of reality. Often there are things that we may want to believe (or not), but 'the truth will out' and we have to confront the way things are, not just the way we may want them to be. It was truth that confronted the disciples on that first Easter morning when the women rushed from the empty tomb. In my own life, it was truth that confronted me some twenty years ago when I was a sceptic. But truth on its own is not enough; beauty is also important, because we are not just cognitive beings.

We are people who love and are profoundly shaped by our desires, made in the image of a God who is love.

Taking truth and beauty into consideration, a person becomes a follower of Jesus Christ not by having that ever-elusive 100% certainty, but instead when they realize that following Jesus Christ and having faith in him is truer and more attractive than their current position. Jesus' call to all people is to 'repent and believe the good news' (Mark 1:15). 'Repentance' may be a slightly strange word to modern ears, but it means a head and heart change of direction. It involves relinquishing everything that is contrary to Jesus Christ and his ways and instead turning to believe in him and his gospel and starting to follow him. He is not calling someone from a position of neutrality to 'make a commitment'; he is calling for a change of allegiance because there is no neutral zone.

Equally, Jesus is not calling us to an abstract set of propositions but to a personal relationship. The truth and attractiveness of Christianity is ultimately the truth and attractiveness of Jesus Christ himself. We are not being called merely to know about him or to assent to some doctrinal propositions, but to know him personally. And how could knowing Jesus Christ ever be abstract, given the magnitude of what he has done? He has lived the perfect life that we should live, died the death that we deserve to die for our rejection of God, and risen to new life. He did this for us when the whole architecture of our lives was set up against him. As Scripture puts it:

> At just the right time, when we were still powerless, Christ died for the ungodly. Very rarely will anyone die for a righteous person, though for a good person someone might possibly dare to die. But God demonstrates his own love for us in this: while we were still sinners, Christ died for us.
> (Romans 5:6–8)

It is worth asking whether whatever it is that you are currently living for has shown you this level of commitment. Careers may promise much, social networks may seem enticing, material possessions may whisper to us about significance and security, but have any of these things ever died for us? The hard truth is that, as with the false gods of old, they demand much from us and give little in return. In the end their empty promises turn to ash and we realize that they have taken everything from us and given us nothing in return. Not so with Jesus; he gives up everything for us before we have even given him a second thought.

I wonder how, as you reflect on the different questions we have been grappling with in this book, you would now evaluate the water you swim in and your own commitments. How well do they stand up to scrutiny; how attractive are they? Are they delivering on their promises? How do they compare to Jesus Christ, his claims, the beauty of his life and his teaching?

Wisdom and a life following Jesus

In the book I have majored on the truth and beauty of Jesus Christ, but I do not want to imply from this that following him is a matter of inernal belief only. The earliest description we have of what it means to be a Christian (even before that term was coined) was to be a follower of 'the Way' (Acts 9:1–2). This is instructive, because Jesus always wanted his followers to have an embodied faith, worked out in 'the way' of lives radically transformed by knowing him. I have focused on truth and beauty merely because every book must be narrowed down in its aim if it is to hope to achieve it. However, alongside the perspectives of whether Jesus' claims are true and beautiful, there is one more vital element: 'What practical difference does it make to my life?'

It might seem odd to us in the West today, but when the gospel of Jesus Christ was first proclaimed, the most persuasive apologetic for

Christianity wouldn't have been its truth or its beauty but the lives of Jesus' followers. In the ancient world, philosophers were most commonly evaluated by the lives they lived and the testimonies of their disciples. People then knew something that we have sadly neglected, that truth needs to be lived out in an embodied reality. Strange as it may seem, that's why many Greek philosophers spent hours in the gymnasium honing their bodies to make their philosophy more compelling, and philosophy lectures were frequently delivered in the gym! Of course, an embodied faith is not in reality about the size of your biceps, but even though these philosophers may have distorted the mind–body association, at least they saw its importance.

It was for this reason that the early Christian thinker Augustine of Hippo stressed the relationship between *scientia* (knowledge about historical events and the world) and *sapientia* (wisdom lived out). He argued that both are important, but that *scientia* should serve *sapientia* because ultimately the point of knowing things is to live a wise life of love for God. Think of it a bit like this: if our pursuit of truth speaks to our head, then our pursuit of beauty speaks to our heart and our pursuit of practical wisdom speaks to our body.

Therefore, in this last part of the book, I want to retrace our steps over the preceding chapters and briefly sketch out a few ways in which what we have been looking at works out practically in our lives. I hope that, as we do this, it will also serve as a useful recap on the ground we have covered. Augustine would call this lived-out 'wisdom', but do be aware that he does not quite mean the same thing you and I do when we think of wisdom, that is, sage advice. Instead, he means a life lived well, a life of human flourishing, a life of love for God and others that 'works' and 'works out' in all its various facets. Of course, we will be able to make only a very brief sketch, picking up one practical virtue for each of the previous chapters and giving a sense of the difference it makes to our lives. Equally, we will be able to see only briefly how belief in Jesus Christ forms these virtues in us. To flesh this out properly would mean an entirely new book. But it is also part of your journey from here, because, ultimately, knowing Jesus is never a place we arrive at this side of heaven. It is a pilgrim's journey, a path of learning more about him, appreciating him and loving him more deeply; and walking that out in a life that is increasingly wise.

1 Origins and thankfulness

In chapter 1 on origins we looked at 'Where do you come from?' as a primary question we all must answer to give us a sense of rootedness in a fast-changing world. Breaking down the question, we considered its two parts, our context (where do you come *from*?) and ourselves (where do *you* come from?). We considered the false dichotomy of science versus Christianity and the ways that a Christian and no less scientific perspective gives us both knowledge and wonder. Then we thought about recapturing 'what we are' as divine image bearers and the many human rights that we derive from this, and the risk of losing them if we turn away from this dignified understanding of humanity.

Throughout Scripture, one of the overriding responses to God for his creation is thankfulness. One of the sung refrains of Israel in the Psalms that comes up time and time again is, 'Give thanks to the Lord, for he is good; his love endures forever' (Psalm 106, 107, 118, 136). Thankfulness is about far more than merely being polite – 'Mind your ps and qs' – it is a heart disposition that receives God's gifts in creation as just that – gifts.

It is striking how there has recently been a resurgence of interest in the virtue of thankfulness, but from a secular perspective. 'Practise thankfulness,' we are exhorted, with studies showing that it makes us more positive, causes us to feel better about our life, helps us go to the doctor less, improves relationships and generally improves our well-being.[4] But is the virtue of thankfulness really coherent if there is no one to give thanks to? How can you receive life as a gift if you really believe it is just a result of chance? On the other hand, the regular practice of giving thanks to God for his many gifts actually enhances our enjoyment of those gifts. In the same way that I will enjoy a painting even more if it is painted *for me*, so seeing God's providential hand in the everyday greatly enhances my enjoyment of life.

- Why not try this practice? Last thing each day, perhaps on your own, perhaps with your family, spend a few moments pausing and giving thanks to God for his gifts. It is a simple but life-giving practice.

2 Truth and integrity

In the chapter on truth we thought about our longing for truth but also our wariness of those who claim to have or know the truth because of how frequently this is used as a mask for power grabbing. The facts/value dichotomy is proposed as a way to deal with this, but it ultimately fails and opens the door to fake news. Instead, Christianity has an integrated view of truth in which facts and values come together and are united in the person of Jesus Christ. Because Jesus lived in space, time and history, we can assess his integrity and verifiability to see if the good news about him is in fact true. As we do this, however, we need to acknowledge our own complicated relationship with the truth. Too often our problem is not lack of information but lack of inclination to believe the truth. Jesus addresses this by knowing the truth about us and yet not using that for his own ends, to domineer and control. Instead, he loves us and forgives us, thereby enabling us to be uniquely truthful about ourselves.

Such a view of truth forms in us the virtue of integrity. Jesus says, 'Blessed are the pure in heart, for they will see God' (Matthew 5:8), with 'purity of heart' here being less about perfection than about integrity. It is, as Psalm 32 says, the blessing of having no deceit in our spirit. This comes from knowing that God sees me, the real me, warts and all, and still loves me and forgives me. Consequently, I can own my failures without letting the shame crush me and I have powerful motives to ensure that my life is not duplicitous.

A key area in which to work out this virtue is life online. How easy is it to project an idealized image of yourself online that lacks integrity? How many businesses collect and use consumer information under the guise of 'improving your customer experience', but are actually more motivated by improving their bottom line? Ultimately we need to be realistic about how hard we find it to act with integrity and how pervasive the attitude of 'doing something as long as I can get away with it' really is. Motivated by knowing that God sees everything about me and yet forgives me, we can cultivate two important aspects of integrity:

- First, honesty. Integrity is not about never getting it wrong but about owning our failures, and seeking forgiveness rather than seeking to hide them.
- Second, consistency: acting consistently across different spheres of life. The question 'Who are you when nobody's looking?' sums it up well. This is not some Big Brother 'God is always watching you' ethic driven by fear, but a healthy realism that God is always with me and life is interconnected; ultimately there is no such thing as private sin, just as God will ensure that no good labour is ever done in vain.

3 Morality and love

In chapter 3 on morality, we asked, 'How do we make the world a better place?' We considered the current generation's strong emphasis on justice but noted the problem of competing visions of what a just world actually looks like. Because of this, it is tempting to think of morality as merely a preference and not something objectively binding for all people everywhere. Ultimately, however, such relativism collapses in on itself and fails to account for our deepest intuitions that there really are such things as right and wrong, good and evil. In Jesus' Sermon on the Mount we see a uniquely balanced and comprehensive vision for a just world that bridges both individual responsibilities and a transformed society, framed by Jesus' evocative phrase, 'the kingdom of heaven'. But this 'kingdom', although attractive, is profoundly uncomfortable, because it exposes our shortcomings. Consequently, we need something more than justice; we need mercy. Jesus' death alone can deal with the tension between our high ideals and our fallen realities, not by sweeping our failures under the carpet, nor by lowering God's perfect standards, but by taking the penalty we deserve for our moral failures and showing us undeserved mercy. This both preserves God's justice and extends forgiveness and restoration to those who fall short.

Such redemption ultimately forms in us the seminal virtue of love and empowers us with that love to work for justice in the world. Jesus teaches that those who have been forgiven much love much (Luke 7:47), and that such forgiveness causes 'rivers of living water' to flow from within them (John 7:38). One of the great problems in pursuing justice is what is known as 'virtue fatigue' or, in a time of emergency, 'crisis fatigue': there is an initial flurry of activity helping others, doing the right thing, resolving to be a force for good, but after a while we find ourselves getting weary, feeling overwhelmed, and it becomes much harder to sustain the same level of love. This was a widely experienced phenomenon during the COVID pandemic. But the gospel addresses such fatigue and cultivates love. First, by mitigating our sense of being overwhelmed by the problems we see because Scripture reminds us that ultimately God is in control and is bringing about a just world, where evil and suffering will not have the last word. Second, when we grow weary of loving others and seeking justice, the gospel renews us. As we reflect on the magnitude of what Jesus has done for us and his unparalleled love, it makes us more loving people and turns us out towards others, seeking their good and working for justice.

- Why not pause and reflect on one or two opportunities in your life where you could act with love and be an agent for change in the world?
- If you have grown weary of doing good, how does reflecting on Jesus' love for you renew your motivation?

4 Happiness and joy

Looking at happiness, we thought about our pursuit of happiness in the West and how we so readily assume that happiness *should* be the supreme good shaping everything from our economy to politics, morality and our views on mental well-being. But our pursuit of happiness has led to a paradox. We have higher life satisfaction scores than before but ever-increasing rates of sadness, worry and anger. So is happiness actually the right thing to pursue? Much of our pursuit of happiness has been bound up with our pursuit of liberty, because we believe that if we remove barriers then we can be 'free to be happy'. But being free from constraints is only as meaningful as knowing what we are to use that freedom for. This is where we really struggle. We have lost sight of what is ultimately valuable and worth pursuing. Scripture frames this as what we worship (literally 'worth-ship') and it is the consistent teaching of the Bible that if we worship idols (anything apart from God), we will never be satisfied. They are 'broken cisterns' (Jeremiah 2:13) that promise much but ultimately have nothing in them to quench our thirst. But when we realize that God alone is ultimately valuable and worth pursuing then we discover a profound truth: happiness is not found in its own pursuit but by pursuing him who is ultimately valuable. In fact this leads to something even deeper and richer than happiness – joy.

Joy transcends circumstances because it is something available even in the midst of difficulty and sadness. If our emotional well-being is defined by a certain set of favourable circumstances – respect from peers, being well thought of, the right career, good health or material prosperity, for example – then our happiness will constantly be in flux and at the whim of a capricious world. If, however, our emotional centre is fixed on God who never changes, then we can know joy whatever the circumstances. The joy of a relationship with the one who loves us and will never leave us or forsake us. The joy of knowing we are forgiven. The joy of a certain and glorious future that is immeasurably better than even the best this world has to offer. The joy of knowing that God will work in all things in our life for our good.

- Why not seek to understand what your heart is attached to by doing the following exercise? Every day for the next week, score your happiness out of 10. Now reflect on what was causing its rise and fall.
  - What has this revealed about what you are living for?
  - In contrast, what would it look like to find your joy in a relationship with Jesus Christ as an anchor for your soul in an ever-changing world?

5 Identity and authenticity

In chapter 5 we started by acknowledging how important identity is as the lens through which we view everything else. We looked at the two prevailing identity narratives, 'Be true to yourself' and 'Be whoever you want to be', and found that they are mutually exclusive because it can't be true both that there is a fixed 'you' to be true to and that you are a blank canvas who can be whoever you want to be. The tension between these narratives is played out in the important but polarized debates about minority group rights. Behind these narratives are desires for liberty and security. Traditional identities offered security but were constraining; more modern identities are liberating but too unstable to build the architecture of our lives on. Jesus Christ, however, offers us both a liberating and a secure identity and this uniquely leads to authenticity.

Authenticity is frequently rated as the most sought-after virtue in this generation. One of the challenges each person faces in the quest for authenticity is to sift through the different parts of 'me' and to work out what is really me and what needs to change. 'You are wonderful just the way you are' may sound attractive as a slogan but it is unlivable in meaningful relationships and if one wants to foster a cohesive society, because it prevents a dynamic of growth and a willingness to change for the sake of others. But how can I know what to change and what to keep? What are appropriate limits to my freedom of self-expression and what are unreasonable constraints?

The good news of the gospel is not that God's grace replaces our nature but that it restores nature. If grace merely replaced nature then every Christian would be a carbon copy, strait-jacketed into submission. Much of the modern world's reaction to Christianity is shaped by this fear that to become a Christian is to have one's identity and diversity crushed (think of the book and TV series *The Handmaid's Tale*[5]). In reaction, we have swung to a libertarian 'grace leaves nature well alone'! But Jesus does not come to replace our nature; he comes to restore it. Because he loves us personally, he wants to make us more fully 'us', more authentic. This is not a move backwards to some past ideal but a move forwards, taking the different parts of who we are – personality, life experiences, relationships, failures, successes – and working through them to restore us to our full potential.

Think of it like this: in my church we have a precious antique – our Communion table. More than two hundred years old, it is very beautiful, with a wonderful inlay of a dove. A few years ago we wanted to restore it. The furniture restorer had a delicate job. He didn't return it to its original colour, because that would have been to negate its history. Its restored colour was deeper, giving a sense of its age. He did polish out the scratches; some dents needed to be filled in, some were left unfilled – polished over but still there as reminders of its story. When fully restored it was a wonderful reminder of the original but it also embodied its two-hundred-year history. And of course there's no way to fake that. A keen observer would always be able to spot a new table that's merely been 'aged' as an inauthentic fake. So it is with Jesus' grace restoring our nature. He loves us and meets us where we are, but he doesn't want to leave us where we are. He is the master restorer, able to work with us carefully to accentuate our strengths, address our weaknesses, polish up the shine of our gifts and fill in our character gaps. By his Spirit he will patiently take a lifetime to do this, each step of the way helping us to become more authentically 'us'. The end result will truly be us, but not as we have yet been; we will be restored by God's grace and yet each will be different, individual and glorious, our authentic self.

- What difference does it make to know that God loves you and accepts you as you, in all of your diversity and individuality?
- What are the areas of your life where you know you need to change to become more authentically you?

6 Hope and being hopeful

Our final chapter was on hope and, unsurprisingly, its corresponding virtue is being hopeful. Hope is different from optimism because it carries within it the sense of a reasonable expectation of fulfilment. We considered that hope is like house keys: put them in the wrong place and you'll lose them. I suggested that, as a culture, since the Enlightenment we have put our hope in humanity and therefore have lost it. Humanity may be able to accomplish much but we cannot carry the weight of our own expectations. Much of our nostalgia and fear when we look to the future evidences this.

The way to recover hope is to steer a careful path between the twin dangers of naivety and cynicism. Naivety dashes hope on the rocks of reality; cynicism breaks it on the rocks of despair. But the resurrection of Jesus Christ is the uniquely hopeful event because it engages with the hardest parts of reality and the darkness of despair. Jesus' resurrection took place in the tomb, the place of death. It is not some 'wishful-thinking' fairy tale but an event in space, time and history, confronting the painful realities of human sin, loss and death. But because the resurrection took place in the tomb it penetrates despair. Many are realistic but have no hope, but if the resurrection can turn even the worst moment in human history into glory, then despair is chased away. This sudden turnaround, this 'good catastrophe', as Tolkien described it, becomes the turning point of human history.

Ultimately, then, hope is cultivated not by mere wishful thinking nor by seeking to have a Pollyanna-like disposition, but by an encounter with the resurrection.[6] We need to let the facts of the resurrection and the wonder of it argue with our hearts. In the seminal chapter on hope in the New Testament, the Apostle Paul reasons thus:

> And if Christ has not been raised, our preaching is useless and so is your faith. More than that, we are then found to be false witnesses about God … And if Christ has not been raised, your faith is futile; you are still in your sins. Then those also

who have fallen asleep in Christ are lost. If only for this life we have hope in Christ, we are of all people most to be pitied. But Christ has indeed been raised from the dead . . .

(1 Corinthians 15:14–20)

Do you notice the confrontation with reality, the careful exploration of the implications of the facts and the counterfacts? This is how we cultivate hope: we seek to locate it in Christ and his resurrection, and that makes us realistic about ourselves and the world around us and also hopeful. When we are fearful about the future, or rocked by present circumstances, we can know that the belief that 'good will win' and 'things will work out in the end' is not a mere platitude or naive optimism but an inescapable implication of God's intervention in Jesus Christ and his resurrection. This energizes our labours and it strengthens our hearts as we embrace the hope of Jesus Christ.

- What things are you fearful of in the present or in the future? How have they affected your hope?
- Whether you believe it (yet) or not, as an exercise of imagination, what difference would it make to how hopeful you are if the resurrection of Jesus Christ were true?

Seeking and saving the lost

In the first chapter I claimed that we have lost the central place of God in our lives. This is an ambiguous use of 'lost'. Have we lost it for good or have we merely misplaced it for a time, with the hope of restoration? A big part of the good news in the Bible is that God is consistently portrayed as the one who 'came to seek and save the lost' (Luke 19:10). Therefore, we are thinking about loss with the hope of restoration. As we've seen, three of Jesus' best-loved parables are about this restoration: the parable of the Lost Sheep, the parable of the Lost Coin and the parable of the Lost (or Prodigal) Son – you can find them in Luke 15:1–32.

The first two parables, of the Lost Sheep and the Lost Coin, both view loss and restoration from God's perspective. Far from his being detached or removed, the stories present God as the seeker, the one who goes to great lengths to find the lost. Jesus asks an intriguing question in the parable of the Lost Sheep:

> Suppose one of you has a hundred sheep and loses one of them. Doesn't he leave the ninety-nine in the open country and go after the lost sheep until he finds it?
> (Luke 15:4)

The surprise in his rhetorical question is that the original hearers would have thought, 'No!' Shepherds in the first century were there partly to lead the sheep to the right places to graze, but also to protect them from wild animals such as wolves, stray dogs and bears. Therefore, a responsible shepherd would never leave ninety-nine sheep unprotected 'in the open country', vulnerable to attack, just for the sake of one errant sheep. The risk would be too great. Not, that is, unless that sheep was particularly precious to the shepherd and was worth the risk. And that really is the point. God seeks those who are lost, who have lost the central importance of him in their lives, because he thinks it is worth the risk, because you are worth the risk. That is why there is such joy when the sheep is found. That is what God has done; that is how committed he is to seeking and saving the lost.

As I close, may I ask, where does this leave you?

The third parable in the trio is the famous one of the Prodigal Son. Unlike the other two parables, it views loss and restoration from *our* perspective. The turning point in this tale is when the lost son 'came to his senses' and decided to return home. This is the other side of the coin. On the one side God is seeking those who are lost; on the other it requires us to come to our senses and to make a decision to return home. Of course, this isn't easy. If you read the parable you can see that it was hard for the son, trudging along the road, rehearsing his apology speech, awaiting the inevitable shame of admitting he was wrong. But then his father spied him from 'a long way off' and the unthinkable happened. The father ran to him, threw his cloak around him, hiding his shame, put his own ring on his finger, restoring his dignity, and they rejoiced. This reception was far more than the son could ever have dreamt of and far more than he deserved. That's the nature of God the Father's love.

I wonder what the road back might look like for you. Perhaps there was a place for God inside you all along . . .

Notes

Introduction

1 'Stressed nation: 74% of UK "overwhelmed or unable to cope" at some point in the past year', Mental Health Foundation UK, 14 May 2018: <www.mentalhealth.org.uk/news/stressed-nation-74-uk-overwhelmed-or-unable-cope-some-point-past-year>.

2 Jeremy Atack and Fred Bateman, 'How long was the workday in 1880?', *Journal of Economic History,* 52(1) (1992): 129–160; Max Roser, 'This is how working hours have changed over time', World Economic Forum, 18 May 2018: <www.weforum.org/agenda/2018/05/working-hours>.

3 J. M. Twenge, 'Are mental health issues on the rise?', 12 October 2015: <www.psychologytoday.com/gb/blog/our-changing-culture/201510/are-mental-health-issues-the-rise>; 'Mental health of children and young people in England, 2017', NHS Digital: <https://digital.nhs.uk/data-and-information/publications/statistical/mental-health-of-children-and-young-people-in-england/2017/2017>.

4 George Monbiot, 'Neoliberalism is creating mental illness. That's what's wrenching society apart', *The Guardian,* Opinion section (12 October 2016).

5 Barry Glassner, *The Culture of Fear: Why Americans Are Afraid of the Wrong Things* (Basic Books, New York, revised edition, 2010).

6 Heinz Bude, *Society of Fear* (Polity Press, Oxford, 2017), p. ix.

7 Glassner, *The Culture of Fear,* p. xix.

8 'UK employment hits another record high', BBC News, 19 February 2019: <www.bbc.co.uk/news/business-47290331>.

9 Jonathan Sumption, 'Coronavirus lockdown: We are so afraid of death, no one even asks whether this "cure" is actually worse', *The Sunday Times*, 5 April 2020.

10 Matthew Arnold, 'Dover Beach'. Accessed online from Poetry Foundation: <www.poetryfoundation.org/poems/43588/dover-beach>.

11 With thanks to Simon Barrington and Rachel Luetchford at Forge Leadership for letting me piggyback on their survey. The survey asked 442 leaders, born between 1984 and 2000, with respondents split evenly between men and women. The wider results and limitations of the survey are written up in Barrington and Luetchford, *Leading the Millennial Way* (SPCK, London, 2019).

1 Origins

1 Amanda Mukwashi, *But Where Are You Really From? On Identity, Humanhood and Hope* (London: SPCK, 2020).

2 Ian Sample, 'Nasa mission to map Mars interior will launch this weekend', *The Guardian*, 4 May 2018.

3 G. K. Chesterton, *Tremendous Trifles*. A Digireads.com Classic, chapter 1.

4 'Chairs are like Facebook' – original advert available at: <www.youtube.com/watch?v=SSzoDPptYNA> (April 2014; original advert released 2012).

5 Charles Dickens, *Hard Times* (Penguin Popular Classics, London, 1994), chapter 2.

6 Charles Taylor, *A Secular Age* (Belknap Press of Harvard University Press, Cambridge, MA, 2007). See for example p. 38: 'As a bounded self I can see the boundary as a buffer, such that the things beyond don't need to "get to me", to use the contemporary expression.'

7 Mary Shelley, *Frankenstein* (Alma Classics, London, new edition, 2014).

8 Alfred North Whitehead, 'The Influence of Western Medieval Culture upon the Development of Modern Science', in *Science and*

the Modern World, Lowell Lectures (New American Library, New York, 1959), pp. 10–22.

9 See for example this list of Christian Nobel laureates: <https://en.wikipedia.org/wiki/List_of_Christian_Nobel_laureates#Physics>.

10 'First worldwide survey of religion and science: No, not all scientists are atheists', Rice University, 2015: <https://phys.org/news/2015-12-worldwide-survey-religion-science-scientists.html>.

11 Albert Einstein, 'Science and God', *The Forum* 83 (June 1930), pp. 373–374.

12 Boethius, *The Consolation of Philosophy*. Independently published. Translated by H. R. James, 2019, p. xiv.

13 Richard Dawkins, *River Out of Eden: A Darwinian View of Life* (Phoenix, London, 2001), p. 155.

14 Johann Chapoutot, *The Law of Blood: Thinking and Acting as a Nazi* (Harvard University Press, Cambridge, MA, 2018), p. 27.

15 See particularly chapter XIV in Tom Holland, *Dominion: The Making of the Western Mind* (Little Brown, London, 2019). Or the discussion between Tom Holland and Douglas Murray: 'Tom Holland is taking on the secular humanists. And he's winning', Premier Christian Radio, January 2020: <www.premierchristianradio.com/Shows/Saturday/Unbelievable/Unbelievable-blog/Tom-Holland-is-taking-on-the-secular-humanists.-And-he-s-winning>.

16 Alasdair MacIntyre, *After Virtue: A Study in Moral Theory* (2nd edn, University of Notre Dame Press, IN, 1984), p. 216.

17 Two parts come together here, the value of education and the value of children; French ethicist Pascal-Emmanuel Gobry writes, 'Christianity's invention of children – that is, its invention of the cultural idea of children as treasured human beings – was really an outgrowth of [Christianity's] most stupendous and

revolutionary idea: the radical equality, and the infinite value, of every single human being . . .' From 'How Christianity invented children', *The Week*, 23 April 2015.

18 C. S. Lewis, *The Weight of Glory and Other Addresses* (SPCK, London, 1942).

2 Truth

1 Cynthia Kroet, '"Post-truth" enters Oxford English Dictionary', in Politico online: <www.politico.eu/article/post-truth-enters-oxford-english-dictionary/>.

2 Simon Blackburn, *Truth: A Guide for the Perplexed* (Penguin, London, 2005), p. 29.

3 Hilary Putnam, *The Collapse of the Fact/Value Dichotomy and Other Essays* (Cambridge, MA, Harvard University Press, 2002).

4 David Sharman, 'Readers ignoring facts and heading straight to comments, says digital chief', *Hold the Front Page* (2017): <www.holdthefrontpage.co.uk/2017/news/editorial-chief-worried-by-trend-of-readers-heading-straight-to-the-comments/>.

5 Roy Greenslade, 'How blurring of fact and comment kicked open the door to fake news', *The Guardian*, 9 October 2017.

6 Walter Lippmann, *Liberty and the News* (Transaction, New Brunswick, NJ, 1995), p. 58.

7 Lewis Carroll, *Alice's Adventures in Wonderland and Through the Looking Glass* (First published 1872; this edition Penguin Classics, London, 1998), chapter 5.

8 G. K. Chesterton, *What's Wrong with the World?* (Kindle edition, 2020), Part 1, chapter 6.

9 Dan Ariely, *The (Honest) Truth about Dishonesty: How We Lie to Everyone – Especially Ourselves* (HarperCollins, New York, 2012), p. 31.

10 *Tit-Bits*, a magazine edited by George Newnes. Article published on 18 September 1897 (No. 831 – Vol. XXXII).

11 Dietrich Bonhoeffer, *The Cost of Discipleship* (SCM Press, London, 2006), p. 89.

3 Morality

1 Fyodor Dostoevsky, *The Brothers Karamazov*. Translated by Constance Garnett (Digireads.com, 2017), p. 225.

2 Global Shapers Survey 2017, <www.es.amnesty.org/fileadmin/noticias/ShapersSurvey2017_Full_Report_24Aug_002_01.pdf>.

3 Jonathan Haidt, *The Righteous Mind: Why Good People Are Divided by Politics and Religion* (Penguin, London, 2013).

4 Edward Mendelson, *Moral Agents: Eight Twentieth-Century American Writers* (New York Review Books Collections, New York, 2015), chapter 7.

5 Ibid.

6 C. S. Lewis, *Mere Christianity* (Collier Macmillan, New York, 1960), p. 31.

7 For an extensive treatment of this train of thought, read the historian (and atheist) Tom Holland's book *Dominion: The Making of the Western Mind* (Little, Brown, London, 2019).

8 I am grateful to Tim Keller for drawing out this distinction in *Generous Justice* (Hodder & Stoughton, London, 2010), chapter 2.

9 William Shakespeare, *The Merchant of Venice*, Act IV, Scene 1.

10 Christian B. Miller, *The Character Gap: How Good Are We?* (Oxford University Press, Oxford, 2018). See particularly chapter 3 on 'Helping'.

11 Shakespeare, *The Merchant of Venice*, Act IV, Scene 1.

4 Happiness

1 'Leisure perspectives: Leisure industry trends from around the globe' (KPMG, 2018).

2 Percy Shelley, 'Speculation on Morals', in Laurence S. Lockridge, *The Ethics of Romanticism* (Cambridge University Press, Cambridge, 1989), p. 316.

3 Jeremy Bentham, *An Introduction to the Principles of Morals and Legislation* (1789), chapter 1.

4 Sigmund Freud, *Civilization and Its Discontents*. Translated by James Strachey (W. W. Norton. & Co., New York, 1961), p. 23.

5 See for example the Organisation for Economic Co-operation and Development (OECD) Better Life Index: <www. oecdbetterlifeindex.org/>.

6 'Changing world happiness', World Happiness Report, chapter 2, 20 March 2019: <https://worldhappiness.report/ed/2019/changing-world-happiness/>.

7 Bruce Levine, 'How our society breeds anxiety, depression and dysfunction', *Salon*, 26 August 2013: <www.salon.com/2013/08/26/how_our_society_breeds_anxiety_depression_and_dysfunction_partner/>.

8 G. K. Chesterton, *The Everlasting Man* (reprint of 1925 edition, Martino Fine Books, Eastford, CT, 2010), p. 75.

9 Pascal Bruckner, *Perpetual Euphoria: On the Duty to Be Happy* (reprint edition, Princeton University Press, Princeton, NJ, 2011).

10 Isaiah Berlin first introduced this distinction in his seminal lecture 'Two Concepts of Liberty', Oxford, 31 October 1958.

11 Data taken from Office of National Statistics.

12 Data from The Centre for Social Justice.

13 Oscar Wilde, *The Picture of Dorian Gray* (Wordsworth Classics, Ware, 1992).

14 Neil Postman, *Amusing Ourselves to Death: Public Discourse in the Age of Show Business* (tenth anniversary edition, Penguin, New York, 2005), p. vii.

15 St Augustine, *Confessions*, Book 1, chapter 1, section 1.

16 'Here Is Love'. Attributed to William Rees (1802–83), translated from the Welsh by William Edwards. Source: Hymns to the Living God #212.

5 Identity

1 Søren Kierkegaard, *The Sickness Unto Death*, translated by Alastair Hannay (Penguin Great Ideas, London, 2008), p. 35.

2 Dino-Ray Ramos, 'Eddie Izzard now using "she/her" pronouns: "I just want to be based in girl mode from now on",' *Deadline*, 20 December 2020: <https://deadline.com/2020/12/eddie-izzard-now-using-she-her-pronouns-i-just-want-to-be-based-in-girl-mode-from-now-on-1234659898/>.

3 See for example Caitlyn Jenner's interview with wbur, 24 April 2017: <www.wbur.org/hereandnow/2017/04/24/caitlyn-jenner>.

4 Charles Taylor, *A Secular Age* (Belknap Press of Harvard University Press, Cambridge, MA, 2007).

5 C. S. Lewis, *Mere Christianity* (various editions), Book III, chapter 10.

6 Francis Thompson, *In No Strange Land* in Wilfrid Meynell, *The Works of Francis Thompson: in two volumes* (Burns & Oates, Ltd, London, 1913).

6 Hope

1 Richard Bauckham and Trevor Hart, *Hope Against Hope: Christian Eschatology at the Turn of the Millennium* (Darton, Longman and Todd, London, 1999), p. 52.

2 Natalie Valios, 'The value of animals in care homes', Community Care, 19 January 2009: <www.communitycare.co.uk/2009/01/19/the-value-of-animals-in-care-homes/>.

3 Andrew Delbanco, *The Real American Dream: A Meditation on Hope* (Harvard University Press, Cambridge, MA, 1999), p. 3.

4 For the full text of The Humanist Manifesto II (1973) and that of other humanist manifestos (1933, 2003), see the American Humanist website: <www.americanhumanist.org/what-is-humanism/manifesto2>.

5 R. L. Wilken, *The First Thousand Years: A Global History of Christianity* (Yale University Press, New Haven, CT/London, 2012), pp. 65–66.

6 Aleksandr Solzhenitsyn, *The Gulag Archipelago 1918–1956* (published in English by Éditions du Seuil, 1974).

7 Verlyn Flieger and Douglas A. Anderson, *Tolkien on Fairy-stories* (HarperCollins, London, 2014. First published as an essay by Oxford University Press, 1947).

Conclusion

1 David Foster Wallace, *This Is Water: Some Thoughts Delivered on a Significant Occasion about Living a Compassionate Life* (Little, Brown and Company, Boston, MA, 2009).

2 Martin Heidegger (1975), interview in the documentary *On the Way to Thinking*: <https://04.phf-site.com/2016/11/heidegger-on-way-to-thinking-english.html>.

3 'The power and the glory: Tom Holland', High Profiles, 19 June 2020: <https://highprofiles.info/interview/tom-holland/>.

4 Consider for example the extensive work done by Dr Robert A. Emmons of the University of California and Dr Michael E. McCullough of the University of Miami, e.g. R. A. Emmons and M. E. McCullough, 'Counting blessings versus burdens: An experimental investigation of gratitude and subjective well-being in daily life', *Journal of Personality and Social Psychology* 84(2) (2003): 377.

5 Margaret Atwood, *The Handmaid's Tale* (new edition, Vintage, New York, 1996). TV series 2017–19 created by Bruce Miller.

6 Eleanor H. Porter, *Pollyanna* (first published by L. C. Page, New York, 1913).